Divinely Decadent

Divinely DECADENT

Stephen Calloway
and Susan Owens

Photography by Deidi von Schaewen

Mitchell Beazley

For Jean Floressas des Esseintes

First published in Great Britain in 2001 by Mitchell Beazley,
an imprint of Octopus Publishing Group Limited,
2–4 Heron Quays, London E14 4JP

Project Editor: *Lara Maiklem*
Executive Art Editor: *Auberon Hedgecoe*
Designer: *Emily Wilkinson*
Editor: *Claire Waite Brown*
Proofreader and Index: *Kathleen M. Gill*
Production: *Nancy Roberts and Alex Wiltshire*

ISBN 1 84000 328 6

A CIP catalogue record for this book is available from the British Library

Typeset in Baskerville

Produced by Toppan Printing Co., (HK) Ltd.
Printed and bound in China

RIGHT *Since the earliest times, intricate workmanship, rich decoration and gilding
have been touchstones of opulence; in more recent times we have come to read them as signs
of a delicious, divine decadence.*

PREVIOUS PAGE *In the Parisian apartment of Brizio Bruschi, the most seductive of tie-backs,
a slim gilded hand, holds back a sumptuous, red, fur-trimmed curtain.*

Contents

A
Little History
of
Divine
Decadence

"I like this word decadent; all shimmering with purple and gold"

… wrote the dissolute poetic genius Verlaine. We can picture him, seated at a table in some low Parisian café, his shaking hand reaching uncertainly toward a glass in which the absinthe glows with a malevolent green light. With all the over-excited imagination of the late nineteenth century, he warms to his theme: the word decadent, he says "throws out the brilliance of flames and the gleam of precious stones. It is made up of carnal spirit and unhappy flesh and of all the violent splendours of the Lower Empire; it conjures up the paint of the courtesans, the sports of the circus, the breath of the tamers of animals, the bounding of wild beasts, the collapse among the flames of races exhausted by the power of feeling, to the invading sound of enemy trumpets. The decadence of Sardanapalus lighting the fire in the midst of his women, it is Seneca declaiming poetry as he opens his veins, it is Petronius masking his agony with flowers."

However much Verlaine's febrile evocation of decadence is steeped in that fierce exoticism so relished by *fin-de-siècle* artists and writers, no matter how much it drips with intimations of lust and cruelty and of other, perhaps yet stranger, sins, it still remains a traditional, even old-fashioned interpretation, based upon the notion of the inexorable decay of ancient civilizations and the fall of empires. For by Verlaine's day there was another, equally well-established, but entirely novel idea of decadence. The new *décadent* was a thoroughly modern figure, chic and sophisticated, self-conscious and highly aware of the importance of attitude and pose. Bohemian or *mondain*, poet, painter or man of letters, aesthete or *flâneur*, the new *décadent* was a superb self-creation, a creature of wit and intellect, one who honed his sensibilities and whose works were, as it was said by the English symbolist poet Arthur Symons, "characterized by a great refinement or subtlety of style and by a marked tendency toward the artificial or abnormal …"

How did this extraordinary transformation come about? How did the idea of decadence, once the doom of exhausted races and crumbling nations, come to be seen as a mark of exquisite refinement, the name carried like the subtly secret badge of an exclusive cult? The very idea of decadence seems deeply embedded in our psyche. As a concept it has taken many twists and turns and its history, reworked in every age, is an intriguing one.

PREVIOUS PAGE *Lillian Williams uses her celebrated collection of French furniture, textiles and other objects to create a modern evocation of the luxury and decadent languor of French aristocratic life before the Revolution.*

RIGHT *The seductive colour and rich furnishing of North African houses has long exerted a charm for Europeans. Franca and Carla Sozzani employ coloured glass, deep saturated wall colours and embroidered silks to create an Arabian Nights fantasy in Marrakech.*

Nearly all the world's great civilizations appear to have been tinged with a kind of pessimistic nostalgia; almost all have looked back to a "dream time," a lost "golden age" or an heroic period of greatness. The Romans in the days of their late splendour feared what they called *inclinatio*, or decline. They sensed that the purity of their spirit, the old strengths and essential nobility of an earlier age were slipping away, that their emperors had become debauched and that, as a sign of this decay, artists and craftsmen could no longer equal the levels of perfection achieved by their ancient predecessors. As a result the most discerning of Roman art collectors despised the sculptors of their own day, prizing original Greek figures above any contemporary work. In spite of a love of the exotic, the old – and self-proclaimingly noble – Romans feared most of all the effects of contact with alien, indulgently "feminine" cultures, especially the louche Orientals and Africans of the conquered provinces, and what they foresaw as the inevitable contamination of their ancient, "manly," martial and public virtues. This was, in reality, a greater fear than that of the "barbarians at the gates."

As in all ages, what we know of the furnishing of the houses and palaces of Rome and the activities of aesthetes and collectors can be read as a sure guide to the tenor of the times. In 1900 – in another era of decadent opulence – Lazenby Liberty, the founder of the Regent Street emporium and a much-courted expert on the decorative arts, observed in a lecture that "during the later Republic and under the Emperors, the luxury and extravagance of every phase of social life was reflected in the furniture. Cicero, who cannot be accused of being a corrupt or particularly ostentatious citizen, gave £9,000 for a table of rare African wood … In the case of the later Roman period … we read of tables of lapis lazuli, with legs of solid gold. This prodigality," he concludes ominously, "had its natural consequence …"

It was the early Christian theologians who first made the direct connection between decadence and sin. From St Augustine onward patristic writers elaborated a complex moral system that built upon the old notion of the pagan virtues, added to these new Christian ones, and formally opposed them to a set of equivalent vices. These vices (all supposed defects of character rather than infringements of doctrinal correctness) came to be codified as the Seven Deadly Sins. Mankind was held to be assailed by the temptation to all of these sins, but it was also recognized that each of us has a "besetting sin," one of the seven to which we are especially susceptible. As a yardstick for the judgment of individuals and as a way of characterizing families, groups and whole nations, this has proved an enduring system.

For centuries, throughout Europe and the Europeanized world, preachers thundered about sin. Rather more entertainingly, writers used the idea of the seven deadly sins as an incisive tool with which to probe the mysteries of human character, while artists depicted both the virtues and the deadly sins in symbolic or more

RIGHT *The Parisian designer Philippe Model created his ruined palazzo effect within the unpromising walls of a redundant 1970s bank building, installing panelling, chimney-pieces and other architectural fragments salvaged from his old family home.*

particularized ways. Not perhaps entirely surprisingly, it is often sinners rather than saints that have proved the most fascinating subjects. The admission of John Wesley, the founder of the Methodist movement, that "The Devil has all the best tunes" has its more decadent echo in Oscar Wilde's deliciously paradoxical maxim "Wickedness is a myth invented by good people to account for the curious attractiveness of others." To this we might add that the most exquisite of rooms, the finest palaces and the greatest collections have often, throughout history, been the creations of the "great" and the "not-entirely-good."

There have been those who lived extravagant, profligate, even sinful lives throughout the centuries, but it was not until the eighteenth century that the idea of a life of physical ease and aesthetic delight became to many an acceptable aim. In France, for the first time since ancient times, the gratification of the senses became an acceptable pursuit. In 1716, Voltaire penned bright and optimistic lines to a friend. "Pleasure," he observed, "is the object, the duty and the goal of all rational creatures." But a darker, obverse side to that coin is to be discerned in the murky thoughts of that stage villain of the Age of Reason, the Marquis de Sade, who wrote "The happiest state will always be that in which depravity of manners and morals is most universal." In later years Voltaire withdrew from what he increasingly viewed as the ugliness and hypocrisy of everyday life into a refined cynicism. "Don't hope to re-establish Good Taste" he wrote to his confidant La Harpe, "we are in an era of the most horrible decadence."

If vice and virtue were often perceived to be in rather gentle competition in the eighteenth century, by the nineteenth the pendulum swing from one extreme to the other had become more exaggerated. On the one hand nineteenth-century morality was severe, unforgiving and (almost to a sinful degree) puffed up with a sense of its own self-importance. On the other, the middle years of the century saw the emergence of the new decadent sensibility. In 1847, Thomas Couture, the American painter, exhibited *The Romans of the Decadence* at the Paris Salon. This scene of ancient mayhem was accompanied with a quotation from Juvenal, the poetic scourge of late Roman morals: "Luxury has fallen upon us, more terrible than the sword, and the conquered East has revenged herself upon us with the gift of her vices." To a middle-class public easily affronted by any suggestion of immorality or depravity and to a new kind of bohemian writer and artist anxious to *épater les bourgeoises*, such a picture gave out very different messages. In an era when the choice of architectural style – ancient or modern, Gothic or classic – was a highly politicized question and in which fervent moral and religious beliefs were brought into play even in judging the decoration of a room, art and literature had a power to shock. That the new aesthetes and bohemians might pursue dubious and decadent ideals or proclaim themselves to be "decadents," was enough to cause widespread alarm.

RIGHT *Surreal and fantastic objects, including some bizarre creatures, are grouped by Brizio Bruschi against an opulent backdrop evoking nineteenth-century button-quilting, and one of his own paintings.*

The French Romantic poet Gérard de Nerval summed up the ideals of the earlier nineteenth-century decadents: "Our period was a mixture of activity, hesitation and idleness; of brilliant Utopias, philosophical or religious aspirations, vague enthusiasms … boredom, discord and uncertain hopes. Ambition was not of our age … and the greedy race for position and honors drove us away from spheres of political activity. There remained to us only the poet's ivory tower where we mounted ever higher to isolate ourselves from the crowd." Of all the poets, it was Charles Baudelaire whose strange imagination would haunt the century. In an introduction to the 1868 edition of his collection of poems, *Les Fleurs du Mal*, Baudelaire's friend Théophile Gautier caught their disquieting flavour of "morbidly rich tints of decomposition, the tones of mother-of-pearl which freeze stagnant waters, the roses of consumption, the pallor of chlorosis, the hateful bilious yellows, the leaden grey of pestilential fogs, the poisoned and metallic greens smelling of sulphide of arsenic … and all that gamut of intensified colours, correspondent to autumn, and the setting of the sun, to over-ripe fruit and the last hours of empires."

For the decadent, dandified aesthetes of the late 1890s the pursuit of beauty, the cult of the obscure and the refinement of the senses were all. Whether in exquisitely jewelled poetry and lapidary prose or in the decoration of their rooms, they sought above all to create an arcane atmosphere untainted by the touch of the vulgar, quotidian world. "As for living," wrote Villiers de l'Isle Adam in his 1886 play *Axël*, "our servants will do that for us." Oscar Wilde caught this nuance precisely when he joked, in his 1889 dialogue *The Decay of Lying*, about an imaginary society. Cyril asks Vivian, the languid aesthete, "Whom do you mean by 'the elect'?" His friend replies "Oh, The Tired Hedonists of course. It is a club to which I belong. We are supposed to wear faded roses in our buttonholes when we meet, and to have a sort of cult for Domitian. I am afraid you are not eligible. You are too fond of simple pleasures." Wilde could never resist the humorous tease, and yet he, too, was one of the most ardent devotees of *A Rebours*, the novel published in 1884 by Joris Karl Huysmans that is widely held to be the quintessential expression of the decadent sensibility.

In *A Rebours*, Huysmans describes the life and sensations of a super-subtle aristocratic aesthete, the Duc Jean Floressas des Esseintes. Throughout the book Huysmans describes in fantastic detail the bizarre and often amusingly perverse tastes of his anti-hero, who retires from the mundane world in order to create a rarefied existence devoted to the gratification of the senses. An instant sensation in Paris, it rapidly gained a wider following. Wilde, who read it, perhaps unwisely, on his honeymoon, introduced the book into his 1891 novel *The Picture of Dorian Gray* as the wicked Lord Henry Wotton's favourite reading matter. It was, he said, "the strangest book that he had ever read … It seemed to him that in exquisite raiment and to the delicate sound of flutes, the sins of the world were passing in dumb show before him. Things that he had dimly dreamed of were suddenly made real to him. Things of which he had never dreamed were gradually revealed ..." Another reviewer dubbed the slim but influential volume "the Breviary of the Decadence."

The idea that the word decadent might describe a precious sensibility and a valued aspect of our culture can be dated from this time. Curiously, it coincides with the gradual move toward what almost amounts to a glorifying of the seven deadly sins, toward an acceptance of them, not quite as virtues, but as pardonably venial peccadilloes. In some areas of human activity – the creation of houses, gardens and collections, for example – the ancient vices seemed to have positive qualities: vainglory and covetousness united in the pursuit of beauty; envy engendered emulation; and sloth expressed itself in the quest for comfort and perfect quietude. And thus it has remained. Today decadence seems all the more synonymous with a wonderful, rarefied sensibility, a dandyism of the senses. Arthur Symons, writing of the value of decadence and the pursuit of strange sins, perhaps came closest to defining this sensibility when he said that the aim of the decadent has always been "to fix the last fine shade, the quintessence of things." But, as always, it is Oscar Wilde who must have the last word: "What is termed sin is an essential element of progress. Without it the world would stagnate or grow old or become colourless. Through its intensified assertion of individualism it saves us from the commonplace."

BELOW *Since the 1960s, the artist Niki de Saint Phalle has created many vast sculptural pieces and follies, including her well-known anthropomorphic Nana houses. The interior of her structures, such as this bedroom lined with mirror mosaic, are as unusual as the exteriors.*

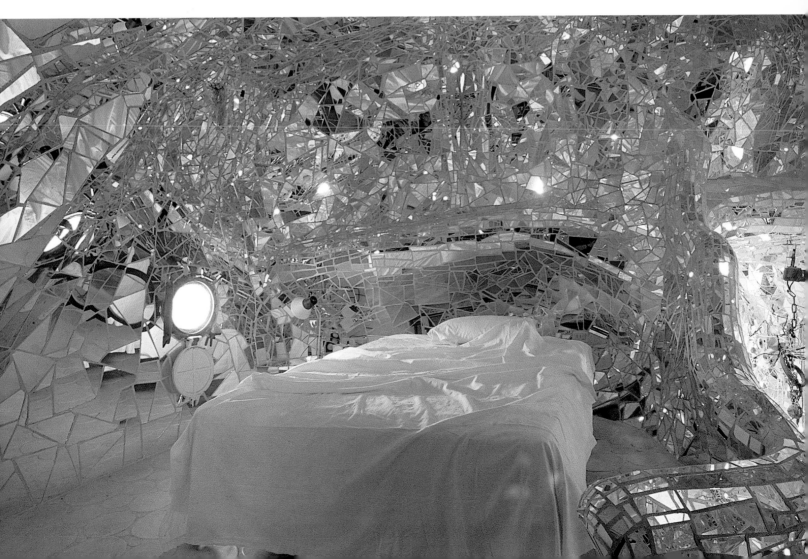

Pride

Chaucer's parson, in lamenting the countless "nombre of harmes that cometh of Pride," describes the ways in which this sin is committed in clothing, sometimes in its "superfluitee," and sometimes, conversely, in its "inordinat scantnesse." The same is perhaps true of interiors. Whether in ostentatious peacock display, where the treasures of a consuming pursuit of beauty are splendidly arrayed, or in the affected chastity and uncompromising chill of a minimalist room, where only the owner's steely self-control is presented for admiration, rooms are invariably the site of this most public of sins.

PREVIOUS PAGE *The evocative charm created when the silvering of old looking-glass decays is impossible to fake. Virginia Bates uses an old pier-glass to reflect the silvery splendour of a cast-iron wash-basin and vanity mirror.*

RIGHT *In Richard Gillette's New York apartment the juxtaposition of a riotously ornate nineteenth-century mirror, faux leopard-skin upholstery and exotic flowers with rough whitewashed brick seems simply to point up the opulence of the furnishings.*

It is from nature that we form our first idea of vanity. In the natural world many species have developed a distinctive physical display or elaborate courtship rituals as the essential means of attracting their mates. Sometimes, as with certain apes, brilliant displays of colour on parts of the body, or the gorgeous feathers sported by many – usually male – birds are sufficient to advertise their availability. Other species, such as lizards with crests that engorge, have developed more startlingly active ways to impress, while others again have perfected alluring dance-like rituals or spectacular postures. The peacock seems to have perfected all three of these aspects of display, uniting them in the unforgettable performance in which the dominant male struts back and forth with his vast array of iridescent tail-feathers held in a shivering, almost menacing fan; this ritual we appropriately refer to as a peacock in his pride.

Curiously, nature also offers us the example of species that take pride in the creation of a setting for their rituals. Many kinds of birds feather their nests as an obvious display of their eligibility; of these, the bower-bird is the doyen of the decorating world, lavishing endless hours upon tricking out its elaborate nest with all manner of brilliant trinkets and found objects in order to add to its allure. The human species has also, over millennia, perfected and codified its forms of display, but, uniquely, mankind in turn has

RIGHT *In Brussels, Agnes Emery has collected classic shaped and bevelled mirrors of the 1920s and 30s and other odd fragments to create a whimsical mirror-room that plays light-heartedly with a theme often found in eighteenth-century rococo interiors.*

FOLLOWING PAGES *Beneath the elaborate eaves of his Secession period villa in Vienna, artist and sculptor Ernst Fuchs has placed one of his own pieces, an extravagant, over life-size gilded bronze symbolic figure.*

LEFT *In an ensemble of old and new decorative pieces in extravagant taste, an exquisite Venetian etched looking-glass is flanked by a pair of candelabra in the form of blackamoor heads on bronze stands by Oriel Harwood.*

RIGHT *In a characteristically surreal touch, jewelled necklaces adorn several of the African game-trophy heads that form part of the decoration of the London restaurant-cum-antique-shop Trois Garçons, created by Hassan Abdullah, Michel Lassere and Stefan Karlson.*

developed a system that limits the degree of personal or domestic ostentation that is considered moral, desirable, or permissible; that which lies beyond this artificially delineated pale has, in almost all societies, been castigated. Although in the Western world vanity and pride have been called sins, they have almost universally proven to be defining factors and spurs to achievement.

All the world's greatest builders have been vainglorious megalomaniacs; their grandiose ideas made solid in brick or hewn stone, their dreams or delusions of power and glory borne up by massive timbers, their craving for everlasting fame carved into intricate patterns or trumpeted with colours and gold. Across the centuries, from the Pharaohs of Egypt who made the most lavish and meticulous plans to lie for all eternity in painted and gilded sarcophagi beneath their great pyramids, through to the vulgar glories of the Sun King, Louis XIV, at Versailles, and so even to the more sinister designs of more recent dictators, pride remains the one great sin that seems triumphantly to possess the power to transcend all others, challenging even death to vanquish it.

On a smaller, but not, in this context, necessarily much more modest scale, absolutely every building ever erected that is more than just a shelter, every room that has been furnished in any way beyond bare utilitarian needs, must owe its very existence to some little act of vanity. Similarly, every collection of objects of any sort that has been brought together has, at some moment, engendered a small swelling of pride in the breast of the collector as they surveyed their achievement.

Even those who have espoused a minimalist aesthetic or a doctrine of rejecting the world wish us to acknowledge their success in the realization of perfect emptiness or to admire the strength of their renunciation of the mundane. For no one who can appreciate

LEFT *Cardinal red walls form a dramatic background for classic modern pieces and a collection of glass candlesticks in the Lisbon apartment of Francesco Capello.*

RIGHT *Bold, modern ceramic pieces and contemporary furnishings, including a standard lamp by Mark Brazier Jones and a red chair, Rose 99, by Masanori Umeda, coexist happily with a nineteenth-century turned rocking-chair. This eclectic mix is anchored by the pale green sheen of the walls and a custom-made carpet.*

the pure, empty and unadorned beauty of a Cistercian abbey can doubt the profound sense of delight and, yes, pride (albeit non-materialistic pride) that such architecture must have given its inmates. In the same way we can sense that even the doctrinaire plainness of the Shaker and Amish lifestyles marked their adherents in their own eyes with a certain, dare we say it, sense of pride, akin to that of today's minimalists, at the self-proclaimingly superior nature of their existence.

The idea of a battle between grandiose display and reticence or restraint is one of the most useful keys to an understanding of the art, architecture and decoration of the modern world. For the last thousand years, overweening self-regard, arrogance and the love of vaunting ostentation have always been demonized by those who are dull and uninspired. Following the teaching of early fathers of the church, pride and its subtler sibling vanity have been denounced as the besetting sins of the great, as well as an ever-present snare to all. Then, as now, of all forms of pride, only civic pride seems to escape the general opprobrium.

In ancient Rome the staggering scale and famed magnificence of Nero's palace, the Domus Aurea, or Golden House, undoubtedly contributed to his fall and the desire of both rulers and citizens of later generations to do all they could to expunge this grandiloquent testament and hated symbol of imperial vanity. By the Middle Ages and well into our own era, riches and proud display remained a vital instrument of power. Kings maintained their position of dominance in part through theatrical pomp; fearing the competition of their rivals, the great Renaissance princes sought to outdo each other in the magnificence of their palaces and the quality of their art collections. In their monumental vanity, Henry VIII of England and Francis I of France each expended unbelievably large sums of money in order to try to eclipse the other's grandeur at their famous meeting in June 1520 on the Field of the Cloth of Gold.

Rulers also feared usurpation by overweening subjects and, therefore, in the interests of power, sought to limit the degree of luxury that courtiers might attain both in their houses and in the gorgeousness of their dress. Court etiquette enforced certain customs, for example that only the king might sit upon a chair with a back, while all others, if they were permitted to sit at all, must use only stools in the royal presence. Strict rules, known as sumptuary laws, also governed the use of rich fabrics and other goods. In December 1546, Henry Howard, Earl of Surrey, fell foul of these edicts; he was arrested and charged with treason. The evidence adduced against him included reports that he had indulged in the outrageous vanity and unlawful luxury of "the wearing of foreign clothes." This extravagance in costume had specifically transgressed the powerful sumptuary laws, which

PREVIOUS PAGES *Lillian Williams' King Charles spaniel takes up a proud stance in one of a set of eighteenth-century French chairs. Brilliantly coloured Chinese wallpaper and boldly bunched lambrequins suggest the opulence of the Louis XV period.*

LEFT *In the cylindrical towers of a disused cement works outside Barcelona, radical architect Ricardo Bofill has carved out the Taller de Arquitectura, his office, workshop and a series of living spaces. The carved chairs are original pieces by Gaudí.*

ABOVE *The exaggeratedly tall, narrow, arched door openings which repeat throughout Bofill's Taller were suggested by original features of the cement works. In the main sitting room, light is filtered through lancet-like windows that pierce the massive walls.*

decreed that earls, dukes and marquises could wear cloth of gold only in their doublets and sleeveless coats, and in no other garments.

In the next century, Louis XIV, proudest and most luxurious of all the monarchs of Europe, used sumptuary edicts in quite a different way, in effect taxing his nobles and keeping them quiescent by forcing them to adhere to strict rules that actually increased the amount of finery they were obliged to exhibit when at court. However, when one subject, the king's treasurer Nicolas Fouquet, appeared to be becoming too fine and too proud – and, it was rumoured, through embezzlement – Louis moved swiftly to break him, seizing for himself the beautiful château of Vaux-le-Vicomte that Fouquet had built and so lavishly furnished. Ironically, however, the French Revolution of 1789 threw down the proud Bourbon dynasty in the person of the mild and ineffectual Louis XVI, thereby opening the way to power for that most vainglorious of upstarts and enthusiastic creators of magnificent palaces, Napoleon Bonaparte.

It may be no coincidence that it was the Napoleonic era that witnessed not only the destruction of the old order in Europe, but also the rise of a new social and artistic phenomenon, the dandy. As *agents provocateurs* of social change, the dandies refashioned vanity, wit and an insouciant attitude to life into a new and totally original pose. For the most part men without property, their subversive aim was to impose upon society a subtle form of vanity based upon style in place of the pride of possession on which the old order rested.

In this way, the most celebrated of the Regency dandies, George Bryan Brummell, known always as Beau Brummell, was famously described as "a nobody who became a somebody, and who ended by giving the law to everybody." He became the ruler of London society and was deferred to in matters of taste, sartorial correctness and elegance by Baronets, Dukes and even the Prince Regent himself. Brummell was essentially a social phenomenon, but it was in France that dandyism first allied itself to the bohemian and artistic worlds, creating an entirely new ideal and philosophy of rarefied existence.

The French poet Charles Baudelaire, himself a dandy, an intellectual and a decadent, defined this startlingly original sensibility: "These beings have no other calling but to cultivate the idea of beauty in their persons, to satisfy their passions, to feel and to think …" He then goes on to explode the vulgar idea that dandyism is simply a matter of lace cuffs and velvet knee-breeches: "Dandyism does not even consist, as many thoughtless people seem to believe, in an immoderate taste for the toilet and material elegance. For the perfect dandy these things are no more than symbols of his aristocratic superiority of mind … Furthermore to his eyes, which are in love with distinction above all things, the perfection of his toilet will consist in absolute simplicity, which is the best way, in fact, of achieving the desired quality."

Today we live in a world in which individual style and attitude have supplanted any fixed canons of taste and old-fashioned ideals of grandeur and authority almost entirely. Personal expression through dress and decoration has become a global obsession, shaping a modern sensibility that owes much to the decadents and aesthetes of the late nineteenth century. As Oscar Wilde put it: "In all unimportant matters style not sincerity is of the essence. In all important matters, style not sincerity is of the essence." And today there are no sumptuary laws; everyone may have at least a little pride in their own style.

PREVIOUS PAGES *Collectors give pride of place in their homes to all kinds of prized possessions. Here, in the Paris loft of the decorator Oddes, unusually, the prized object in the library is an Italian Moto Guzzi bike.*

RIGHT *This opulent fantasy bathroom in the London apartment of Brian Lewis, reminiscent of a chamber in Ludwig of Bavaria's castle at Neuschwanstein, is based on a grotto theme; it follows in the grand European tradition of building unusual, folly-like structures in which to bathe.*

LEFT *Virginia Bates'*
exquisite dressing table
strewn with old silken
flowers seems more redolent
of Proust's evanescent and
fragrant recollections than
of the sere memories of
Dickens' Miss Havisham
in Great Expectations.

ABOVE *Among the most*
inventive of contemporary
designers, Parisian duo
Mattia Bonetti and
Elizabeth Garouste here
transform the classic
elements of dressing table,
toilet mirror and stool into
objects of amorphous fantasy.

Covetousness

Covetousness is central to the decadent character, for the acquisition of rare, strange and gorgeous objects to amuse and stimulate the jaded mind is essential to this restless and uneasy temperament. The breathless exhilaration of the quest, the thrill of capture, the enjoyment of the novelty, all are sensations craved by the febrile aesthete. Yet mere possession soon engenders ennui, a subtle malaise possesses the mind, covetousness gains ground anew and can only be allayed by yet greater extravagance, the acquisition of ever more recherché and esoteric things.

*L*ong before the days of Rome's decadence, collecting ancient Greek sculpture and other works of art had already become something of a mania. Philosophers and poets spoke of the nobility of the desire to surround oneself with beauty, and patrician collectors considered their houses ennobled by antique pieces, but rich merchants and powerful military commanders grew steadily more ruthless as collecting took on a more competitive face. In the third century bc, the fall of Sicily – once one of the richest of the Greek colonies – gave a new impetus to the wholesale ransacking of older settlements for ancient marble and bronze statues. In 212 bc, the triumphant Marcellus signalled his victory at Syracuse by sending a vast shipment of art objects back to Rome; a quarter of a century later Scipio emulated this grandiose gesture when he returned bearing the spoils of Tarentium, including the famous figure of Hercules by Lysippus.

In the mid-first century bc, the Roman governor of Sicily, Caius Verres, was so aggressive in his pursuit of statuary that Cicero, Roman consul, orator and writer, said of this unattractive figure that his desire for art made him a robber and a criminal. The pursuit of beauty has ever been tinged with greed, unscrupulousness and even madness. By the time of Caesar, who enjoyed beautiful things and himself assembled an outstanding collection of intaglio gems and seals, art collecting was well established and specialist merchants had begun to flourish in Rome. They supplied rare original pieces to discriminating connoisseurs who could afford the best, and carried on a lively trade in modern copies, of varying quality, for would-be collectors who lacked an eye for quality or a purse deep enough to pay for it.

Though the Dark Ages were perhaps rather less benighted than we like to paint them, it is nevertheless true that in these years history tells us much of a barbaric love of splendour, of treasure hordes and pillage, and little of collecting and connoisseurship as we understand them.

PREVIOUS PAGES *The collector Alexandre Vassiliev's extraordinary assemblages of nineteenth-century objects, including shoes, shoe buckles and belt clasps, are set against a backdrop that evokes the unmistakably Russian interiors of Pushkin's St Petersburg.*

LEFT *Massing whole groups of similar objects creates a display in which forms echo one another and colours seem intensified, an effect seen here in Hunt Slonem's collection of Venetian and other coloured glass decanters and flasks.*

ABOVE *Philippe Model delights in creating arrangements of unusual objects. Mingled here are pieces of old lead-crystal glass, battered silver, and modern eccentric sculptural pieces of painted cassein, all reflecting dimly in a ghostly, decaying mirror.*

PREVIOUS PAGES *In his Paris loft, David Rocheline creates* a coup d'oeil *not so much with objects but rather by the obsessive massing of pattern on pattern in a contemporary manner that restates the taste of the Second Empire period for overwhelmingly opulent effects.*

LEFT *In his New York apartment, John Woodrow Kelley, beneath his own large, neoclassical-style painting, groups obelisks, ancient seal-casts, marble fragments and a Greek black-figure wine-cup; all classic objects redolent of the taste of eighteenth- and early nineteenth-century grand tour collectors.*

FOLLOWING PAGES *As one of London's most renowned antique dealers, Keith Skeel has also assembled an idiosyncratic personal collection. A vast pine dresser in his kitchen groans beneath an array of nineteenth-century domestic crockery, while a superb group of cheese bells is massed upon the table.*

The appreciation of beauty and the desire to own objects for any reason other than their intrinsic value seems largely to have been confined to a few rare and puissant rulers of unusual sensibility, and otherwise to have been almost a monopoly of the more refined grandees of the church. For several centuries, it seems, almost all domestic buildings – even royal residences – were more or less utilitarian and primarily defensive; beautifying and enriching cathedrals, abbeys and smaller chapels remained the most powerful, if not the sole impetus to the creation of works of art. By a curious twist, this essentially pious response to things of beauty became inextricably linked with the new and growing collecting obsession that increasingly came to drive the medieval church: that of the relics of the saints.

Aside from the spiritual dimension, the possession of important relics could prove to be vastly lucrative to a religious establishment, turning an obscure or humble foundation into a shrine and place of pilgrimage. As a result, the means by which relics were acquired were at times murky and often involved theft, subterfuge and even outrageous fakery. Nonetheless, here was an area in which an extreme and often ruthless covetousness seemed to be no sin. At the beginning of the Middle Ages, the Emperor Charlemagne wholeheartedly encouraged his church in the pursuit of relics. He condoned the often dubious activities of his friend and biographer, the Bishop Einhard, who, with the wealth and encouragement of the emperor behind him, became one of the most enthusiastic relic collectors of his era.

To the faithful, all kinds of relics were worthy of veneration: skulls and bones, and at times the entire bodies of saints were jealously preserved, and had to be carefully guarded against theft by rival churches. Other items, such as pieces of clothing associated with the lives and deaths of saints, were also valued and enclosed in sumptuous reliquaries, while all manner of more curious objects became attractions to the pious. Henry III of England possessed a phial believed to contain the Holy Blood shed at the crucifixion, as well as the Holy Footprint, the supposed last mark left upon earth by Christ at the moment of the Ascension. So-called pieces of the True Cross and Holy Nails were exhibited in relic chambers all across Christendom, and, more bizarrely still, several competing relic collectors claimed

LEFT *In their Parisian house, the celebrated artists and photographers known simply as Pierre et Gilles have assembled a glittering shrine to popular culture and camp taste. Illuminated by the pink glow of fairy lights, this display is strangely reminiscent of Hindu shrines.*

ABOVE *Elevating fragments of trash culture to a heightened significance, a characteristic grouping of kitsch objects in the house of Pierre et Gilles places a pair of camp figurines of mermen – portraits of Pierre et Gilles – against a souvenir model of a lighthouse.*

to possess the authentic Holy Foreskin. By the time of the Reformation, it was this undisciplined greed for relics and their obsessive veneration that were held to be among the most damning signs of the avarice and decadence of the old church.

The obsessive pursuit of art begins with the Italian princes of the Renaissance, such as the Medici in Florence and the Gonzagas of Mantua, who vied with each other to possess the greatest works of antiquity and to commission the finest new pictures and decorative schemes from living painters. North of the Alps, the greed for paintings was matched by an insatiable mania for collecting natural objects, such as rare corals and sea shells, feathers, unusual horns and stuffed or preserved animals, birds and sea creatures. In Cabinets of Curiosities, the forerunners to museums, these rarities were formed into elaborately arranged patterns.

Often next to such a cabinet of natural marvels was to be found the Kunstkammer, in which were gathered examples of ingenious, intricate workmanship and objects made by the most cunning of artificers from rare and exotic materials. Here might be found clocks with elaborate mechanisms, curious carvings and cups made from coconut shells, turned from tusks of ivory, or cut from single pieces of rock-crystal, porphyry, lapis lazuli and other semi-precious stones. In the general lust for possession, strange values were assigned to items in the great princely collections; we know, for example that the Medici placed a higher value upon a narwhal tusk – albeit prized at that time as a unicorn's horn – than on any of the paintings, including the great allegories by Botticelli, that they owned.

Stories of the lengths to which rich and powerful collectors will go in the pursuit of the things they desire create an often alarming index of the insatiability of human covetousness. Christina, Queen of Sweden in the seventeenth century, so lusted after the fabled collections of the tragic Habsburg Emperor Rudolf II, that, in the last days of the Thirty Years War she wrote to her general in the field, Wallenstein, warning him that a peace treaty was imminent and urging him to make all possible speed to sack the city of Prague. Christina's troops torched the city and ransacked and looted the cabinets and galleries of Rudolf's castle palace. They carried back to the north hundreds of paintings and many priceless curiosities and other objects. On the queen's instructions they also seized Rudolf's great library of books and manuscripts, piling everything onto more than a hundred great wagons, but not before tearing off and discarding the superb bindings in order to lighten the load.

A century later, Catherine the Great, Empress of Russia, was no less avaricious in her desire to amass a great collection. Unlike Christina, however, her methods involved the use not of arms but of silver-tongued agents and the inducements of vast sums of money. She bought entire libraries and collections, such as the celebrated gallery of old masters from Houghton Hall, Norfolk, formed by Sir Robert Walpole, the loss of which was considered by English connoisseurs to be a national disaster. Catherine was perhaps more honest than many another insatiable collector when she characterized her own collecting: "It is not for love of Art, it is voraciousness; I am not an amateur, I am a gourmandiser."

William Beckford, famously described as "England's wealthiest son," was also one of the most obsessive and exacting collectors in the history of taste. As an Englishman and an aristocrat, he risked his life to go to Paris during the height of the French Revolution for the chance to buy the finest examples of the work of the French *ébénistes*. As other aristocrats went to the guillotine Beckford travelled in disguise, snatching treasures from scattered

LEFT *Collectors of fashion tend to seek either cool, classic, or more opulent pieces. Eva Fuchs in Vienna has sought out in particular the most exotic and lavish pieces of the earlier twentieth century, gathering heavy costume jewellery, beaded dresses and bizarre shoes.*

RIGHT *A somewhat sinister feeling pervades the group of figures assembled in the Calistoga studio of Ira Jaeger. Created for religious and secular purposes, when grouped together, these varied figures take on a disturbing fascination.*

LEFT *An obsessive collector of furniture, pictures and objects of the 1830s, 40s and 50s, Alexandre Vassiliev imbues the rooms of his Parisian apartment with the perfect, precious* stimmung *(feeling or atmosphere) of his favourite era.*

RIGHT *In an already architecturally imposing space, the painter Stefan Riedl has used spirited trompe l'oeil painting and a collection of highly extravagant pieces of furniture to evoke the decadent opulence of the Vienna of past times.*

FOLLOWING PAGE LEFT *Among the latter-day disciples of Sir John Soane, Peter Hone, as a major dealer in garden sculpture and architectural fragments, has had a unique opportunity to assemble a superb collection of pieces which he has arranged with a consummate eye for placing in his London house.*

FOLLOWING PAGE RIGHT *In a corner of one of Peter Hone's rooms a Roman throne is surrounded by architectural and sculptural fragments. Nothing disturbs the subtle, almost monochromatic colour scheme of stone, plaster and pale, bleached floorboards.*

libraries and bidding for the contents of ransacked châteaux. He acquired priceless pieces by the greatest furniture makers, such as Boulle, and even the most celebrated desk, the Bureau du Roi Stanislaus, the greatest masterpiece of Riesener, rescued from the king's own study.

In the latter part of the nineteenth century and in the early decades of the twentieth, the counterparts of these great collectors of the past were the so-called robber-barons of America, the unbelievably rich and powerful, self-made coal and steel millionaires, railroad bosses and industrialists such as J. Pierpont Morgan. These titans of the new commercial order drew the treasures of the old world in an inexorable flow across the Atlantic. Unlike their great predecessors, however, a great many of these collectors – most notably Morgan himself, but also Henry Clay Frick in New York and Henry Huntingdon in California – in the end turned public benefactors and gave their treasures to the people, either enriching existing museums such as New York's Metropolitan Museum of Art or creating their own foundations. This complex urge to square covetousness with philanthropy has continued in more recent eras with Paul Mellon and John Paul Getty.

Among private collectors today it is intriguing to see how the simple desire to possess beautiful things is so often tinged with something of the ethos of the old relic hunters. Things acquire an extra lustre by their associations. To possess a treasure with provenance, that is to say an object made numinous by a history of having been coveted, owned and valued by previous collectors, adds to collecting the most exquisite piquancy of all; in this most rarefied of sensibilities, surely, is to be found the subtlest quintessence of covetousness.

Lust

Too world-weary for the continual pursuit of sexual conquest, the voyeuristic pleasures of the sequestered decadent are provided by visual and literary delights. The walls are lined with pictures: the exquisite sensuality of Aubrey Beardsley's drawings, the lapidary intensity of Gustave Moreau's watercolours, the harsh eroticism of the prints of Félicien Rops. Heavy leather-bound books of engravings depict cruel couplings and depraved acts; rich furs caressed by languid fingers are reminders of the "horror and ecstasy" felt by Sacher-Masoch's Severin; or the enervated eye can simply rest on nude caryatids, sculpted with high regard for anatomical detail.

*O*f all the old sins, *luxuria* was certainly held to be the most besetting, though not, perhaps, ultimately, the most deadly; that distinction being reserved in the great scheme of things for pride. It was, however, viewed by the early patristic moralists as the most complex of the sins. To them, *luxuria* was an amorphous creature armed with myriad tentacles of temptation. Among its many and various snares were what we should now define simply as the different varieties of pure lust, both mental and physical; but inextricably combined with these were other, more esoteric, abstract and imaginative temptations, such as the overwhelming desire for luxury and magnificence (which of course also verges upon the great sin of pride) and, in particular, the excessive pursuit of comfort.

For the dedicated modern decadent there is a quite delicious irony in the fact that even as late as the sixteenth and seventeenth centuries "magnificence" – that is to say ostentation, and, specifically, the celebration of wealth, power, grandeur and refined taste through conspicuous display – was admired and revered as one of the greatest of the so-called Aristotelian virtues, whereas "luxury" – defined then as the mere craving for all that is over-rich or the undisciplined delight in comfort – was held to be a serious defect of

PREVIOUS PAGES *In a bedroom design by Abu Jani and Sandeep Koshla for Dimpel Kapadia in Bombay, doors made from a sacrificed baroque painting lead to a huge divan reminiscent of those in the art deco palaces built by the last great maharajahs of the 1930s.*

LEFT *Virginia Bates uses trompe l'oeil ceiling painting, perfectly judged pink and peachy tones, and painted and silvered French furniture to recreate the romantic look and heavily scented atmosphere of the boudoirs of the early Hollywood screen goddesses.*

ABOVE *In her drawing room, Virginia Bates has employed painted finishes including faux marble to create the richer effects of the classic French haut-bourgeois decorative style of the late nineteenth century.*

character and, as such, one of the seven great sins. By contrast, in our own era, the very idea of magnificence or any overt attempt or even desire to impress, has come to be demonized as immoral, undemocratic and politically incorrect, while banal material comforts and the everyday mediocrities that now pass for luxury – "luxury homes," "luxury holidays," and even "luxury toilet tissue" – lie within the impoverished expectation of almost all.

Let us then rejoice that in these prosaic days there remains yet at least a small number of aesthetes, decadents and cultured sybarites who celebrate the glories of the ancient entwined ideals of *luxuria*; ardent spirits who still seek beauty and pleasure in sensuousness and sensuality, who maintain in these unpropitious times the fierce desire to revel in grandeur and magnificence on the old scale and who wish still to create for themselves superb and sumptuous surroundings. It is these happy few who retain the key to the delights of the most exquisite pavilion in the palace of the senses.

These seekers after strange sins and rarefied pleasures have rediscovered the ancient secret that it is in the mystic conjunction of lust and luxury that the most exquisite delights are to be enjoyed. By an old alchemy, the lust for luxuries and the luxuries of lust combine to transmute dull, ordinary pleasure into ecstasy. It is in some ways perhaps a similar process to that of theatre, whereby the elements of the play: words, characters and dramatic action, are transformed by the magic of costume, colour, decor and lighting.

For this reason, the decadent will lavish endless pains upon the creation of the perfect stage set for the enactment of the high drama of love and the melodrama of lust. Here then, the lover's chamber becomes a private theatre, in which every element combines to enhance grand illusion and to advance subtly orchestrated action to its theatrical climax. Unlike a real theatre, however, in which the magic of the illusion lives only in the present, the decadent's chamber is also the place for the eager speculative contemplation of, as yet, untasted pleasures, and, perhaps most deliciously of all, for the delicate remembrance of pleasures past, those "moments of emotion recollected in tranquillity" as described by William Wordsworth in the introduction to *Lyrical Ballads* (1798).

The creation of the most rarefied setting for the all-too-fleeting present pleasures of the flesh and for the compelling transports of memory or the fevered imagination can, for the true decadent, for the gourmet of sybaritic indulgence, become, as it became for that quintessential fictional aesthete, des Esseintes, the greatest pleasure of all. In fact, the character and supposed tastes of Huysmans' des Esseintes, were in part modelled on the figure of Robert de Montesquiou, an aristocratic aesthete who spent much of his time in the remodelling of exquisite rooms in his own house, the Pavilion Rose outside Paris. Montesqiou in real life was both a dandy and an exotic; living a charmed existence, he raised the pursuit of art, poetry and a devotion to refined, artificial luxury to a new and previously undreamed of level.

Following Huysmans' superbly inventive and often slyly humourous catalogue of the weird decorations of his hero's rooms in the imaginary Château de Lourps, literature, especially that of the following *fin-de-siècle* decade, abounds in evocations of wonderful rooms and their creators. Among the cleverest is one to be found in *Teleny*, the most infamous novel of its era, and the product of the louchest section of London's literary underworld of the 1890s. It was almost certainly written by several collaborators, one of who it has always been

RIGHT *Virginia Bates has used silks, satins, lace and artificial flowers heaped in profusion upon a pink upholstered daybed to create an opulently feminine atmosphere in which an Edwardian corset seems to become the quintessential decorative object.*

FOLLOWING PAGES *Utilizing the same heightened visual effects that characterize her design work for the New RenaisCAnce group, Carolyn Corben has created an erotically charged bedroom interior with huge photo-enlarged details from paintings such as Bronzino's* Allegory of Time and Love.

LEFT *In the State Bedchamber of his eighteenth-century house, the late Dennis Severs invented a superb bed in the early eighteenth-century style of designer Daniel Marot, using fabric and glue, cords and tassels to dress up a structure based on cut-out shapes and cardboard tubes.*

RIGHT *Approached through a massive stone archway, a brilliant red mattress takes the place of the ancient divan in Franca and Carla Sozzani's reworking of a traditional house in Marrakech.*

said, was Oscar Wilde. Frankly describing several episodes of a "love that dare not speak its name" somewhat incongruously interspersed with passages chronicling more conventional sins, the book, which was never openly published in its time, is now more fascinating for the way in which its unknown authors parallel lust, luxury and minute details of anatomy and interior decoration in precisely depicted rooms:

> it was a most peculiar room, the walls of which were covered over with some warm, white, soft, quilted stuff, studded all over with frosted silver buttons; the floor was covered with the curly white fleece of young lambs; in the middle of the apartment stood a capacious couch, on which was thrown the skin of a huge polar bear. Over this single piece of furniture, an old silver lamp – evidently from some Byzantine church or some Eastern synagogue – shed a pale glimmering light, sufficient, however, to light up this temple of Priapus, whose votaries we were. "I know", he said, as he dragged me in, "I know that white is your favourite colour, that it suits your dark complexion, so it has been fitted up for you and you alone. No other mortal shall ever set foot in it."

Few novelists of the nineteenth century, perhaps not even Dickens in one of his most elevated moments of high seriousness, could so accurately have mirrored action with telling description of setting.

Curiously, in decoration – as in so many areas – it has been the nineteenth century which has fixed our images of decadence. From the descriptions of the silken, cushion-strewn divans in the dusty, gilded rooms of the Hôtel de Lauzun, the old palace on the Ile St Louis in Paris where Charles Baudelaire and his Romantic cronies smoked cannabis during the sessions of the notorious "Club des Haschischins," to wide-eyed journalists' reports of Aubrey Beardsley's predilection for shutting out the day with heavy curtains and drawing by the light from two massive gilded candlesticks, the association between vice and a certain kind of room has become indelibly fixed. As a result, when, in 1907, Elinor Glynn wished to promote the sale of her slightly risqué novel *Three Weeks*, she found the easiest way of attracting attention was to pose in a carefully styled interior that telegraphed to a panting world that here, indeed, was the latest *femme fatale*, a writer, but also a woman capable of every known or unknown vice. She did nothing to suppress the resulting rhyme: "Would you like to sin with Elinor Glynn on a tiger skin, or would you prefer to err with her on another fur?"

This association of decorative opulence with depravity and lust has become commonplace, enshrined, perhaps most obviously, in the styling of Hollywood films and in the fevered, yet oddly hackneyed, imaginations of the writers of tabloid journalism. Much more intriguing is the message signalled by interiors that do not conform to such obvious stereotypes. The extraordinary rooms created by T.E. Lawrence ("Lawrence of Arabia") at Clouds Hill, his little house near Dorchester, are a case in point. The whole house is wierdly idiosyncratic and utterly uncompromising in its decorative features and effects. In his bedroom, Lawrence arranged a strange, and undoubtedly decadently erotic interior in which bookshelves and displays of photographs and other souvenirs of his desert experiences surround a bizarre, or even fetishistic, bed with a brown leather mattress and pillows bearing the Latin words "meum" and "tuum" ("me" and "you").

PREVIOUS PAGES *A spectacular gilded architectural fragment of a sunburst focuses attention on the vast, fur-covered bed of the Trois Garçons, Hassan Abdullah, Michel Lassere and Stefan Karlson.*

RIGHT *In this ancient house in Marrakech, belonging to Alessandra Lippini, the characteristically simple, rustic elements, such as the massive high-posted bed and shaped wall niches, are dramatized by the use of brilliant orange tadelakt, the traditional tinted and polished plaster wall finish of old Moroccan houses.*

FOLLOWING PAGES *In his fantasy house that clings to a lush hillside in Hollywood, the late, great decorator Tony Duquette used exotic elements from many cultures – especially Oriental – fused into a rich, highly coloured and idiosyncratic mix.*

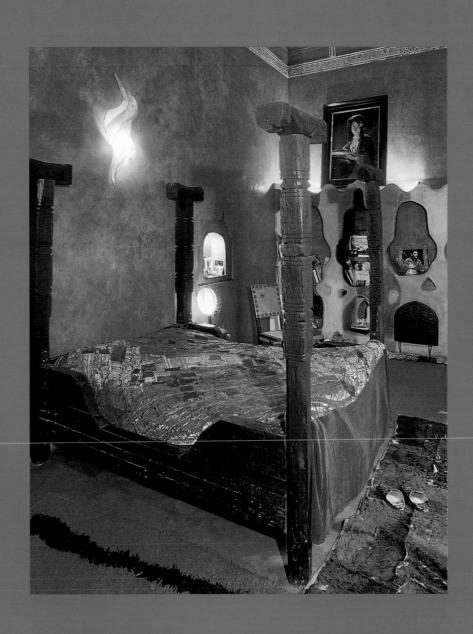

Those few who saw Lawrence's strange rooms at Clouds Hill can have had little doubt that here was a distinctly decadent house, a place of deeper and more bizarre self-indulgence than many a more obvious and opulent creation of the self-proclaimingly decadent "Bright Young Things" of the Twenties. Clouds Hill seemed always touched with a sense of melancholy, wholly suited to its occupant's pose as one who has done with the everyday world.

It was, perhaps, Théophile Gautier, poet, novelist and critic, writing in the preface to the 1868 edition of his friend Baudelaire's *Les Fleurs du Mal*, who caught the essence of this curious alliance between sensuality and sin, decadence, decay, decoration and death:

> The style of decadence is nothing else than art at that extreme point of maturity produced by those civilisations which are growing old, their suns low in the sky – a style that is ingenious, complicated, learned, full of shades of meaning and research, always pushing further … taking colours from all palettes, notes from all keyboards … obscure phantasies at which the daylight would stand amazed.

BELOW *Though coolly minimalist in form, a bedroom in Antonio Presto's Hotel Atelier Sul Mare in Sicily projects a stark, powerful feeling of highly charged eroticism by the dramatic and unexpected use of colour.*

LEFT *One room in the house of the Trois Garçons is devoted to the more unusual pieces of 1960s and 70s furniture they have discovered, such as a weirdly sensuous, vertebrae-like modular sofa. The effect is that of a 1970s seducer's pad.*

FAR LEFT *One of the great innovators of 1960s design, Gaetano Pesce continues to explore the use of novel materials and unusual forms such as in this wheeled, extravagantly upholstered bed. The illuminated chair is one of his classic experiments using glass-fibre and resin.*

Envy

Contempt for the majority of the human race may well be a characteristic of the decadent. Yet, apropos of previous eras, those glittering, seductive, unreachable golden ages of art and poetry, envy and its correlative, emulation are, paradoxically, equally constitutive. Retrospective, nostalgic envy is essential to a state of decline; each age nurtures the fiction of a more glorious past, in comparison to which the present is shabby and vulgar. It is the decadent's self-imposed mission to recreate something of the glory of these past splendours.

We habitually associate the Romans with decadence, and indeed their cruelty, arrogance and love of luxury have, to a great degree, formed the benchmarks of that aspect of the decadent sensibility. However, their national character was moulded by an uneasy envy of the civilization of the ancient Greeks, and a deep desire to emulate it in as many ways as possible. Much that we see as coarse and vulgar in the Roman way of life and culture was no more than a debased reflection of Greek skills, virtues and accomplishments as Rome perceived them. Beyond the simple wish to imitate the style of Greek life and copy its details, for the most cultured Romans their greatest desire was to recreate the perfections of what they had come to cherish as a lost golden age. The idea of Arcady, one of the most persistent threads of our civilization, is one essentially tinged with nostalgia. In very different ages, Sir Philip Sidney's Elizabethan poem *Arcadia*, the classical landscapes of Poussin and Claude and the English garden of the eighteenth century are all heartfelt evocations of this same melancholic sentiment, just as, in more recent times, Aubrey Beardsley's images of pierrots and fauns, the music of Debussy and Rex Whistler's wistful and whimsical neo-rococo mural paintings can all be seen as yearnings in their own ways for the lost idyll.

PREVIOUS PAGES *Stefan Riedl has collected massive pieces of gilded furniture and chandeliers, and used his own bravura trompe l'oeil painting to great effect, evoking the heavy baroque grandeur of the old town palaces of Vienna in an enfilade of rooms.*

LEFT *The dense, yet still delicate, arabesque decoration of a bedroom in the house of the Comtesse Boul de Breteuil in Marrakech recalls the exquisite wall treatments of the palace apartments of the Alhambra.*

ABOVE *In her desire to create her own version of French eighteenth-century aristocratic life, Lillian Williams has gathered many superb pieces, such as this lit à la Polonaise, which she has draped authentically in the manner to be seen in many paintings of the period.*

This nostalgia and *tristesse* lies at the very heart of the decadent sensibility. Every age searches for its own ideal precedent: Renaissance artists and their scholarly patrons believed that they were rediscovering the old architectural secrets and reawakening the learning of the ancients. Sixteenth-century Mannerism is in turn a debased emulation, a bizarre crepuscular reflection of the shining ideals of the Renaissance dawn. The rococo, the least muscular of styles, plays a decadent, whimsical game, subverting the bold rigour of the baroque. The nineteenth century ransacked the past like a dressing-up box, trying on every style, seeking at one moment the ancient virtues in neoclassicism and, at the next, the romance of a colourful, chivalric past in the quaintness of the gothic revival.

This nostalgic impulse found concrete expression in many media and in all branches of the arts. Yet its most fascinating form is represented by the architectural folly. The definition of the folly makes obvious its decadent character, for its *raison d'être* lies in a capricious and knowing play upon an original theme, taking a building and creating a mannered copy of it divorced from its original context, freewheeling amidst decorative effects and thereby creating a new and entirely personal atmosphere for the enjoyment of those who understand the game and appreciate its subtleties. For learned eighteenth-century gentlemen architects, the idea of copying, but investing the copy with either humour, a new poetic pathos, or simply an unlikely use, represented the very height of what the period defined as wit. All manner of structures began to appear: Piranesian ice-houses, shell-grottoes, rustic seats, pagodas, gothic menageries, tea pavilions in the chinoiserie manner and Moorish tents of painted tin all vied with Greek Doric temples, Roman triumphal arches and Egyptian obelisks in an extraordinary battle of the styles.

In particular, the fashion for artificial ruins tells us much about the ideals of those eighteenth-century English milords whose taste was formed while making the grand tour. For these connoisseurs, the ruined remains of classical civilization became imbued with an aetheticized, intellectual charm that found a sort of minor-key echo in the more melancholy and poetic remains of gothic ruins at home. Returned to England, with ambitious plans to build classical houses and to lay out their parks in the new, picturesque manner, their thoughts turned naturally to the creation of landscape features and appropriate garden temples, grottoes and other devices. What is intriguing here is the rapid growth of a somewhat decadent fondness for antique corruption and "pleasing decay" which is an entirely novel aspect of the taste of the era, and which is seen at its most delightful in the many sham ruins built by eighteenth-century grandees as "eye-catchers" to complete a view or as places for quiet contemplation. Certainly the most bizarre and decadent of these artificial ruins were the ones built in the form of collapsing gothic chapels and for which the proprietor hired a "hermit" to be shown to visitors. Like any other retainer, these hermits were paid a wage; in return they were required to wear a monastic habit, allow their hair and fingernails to grow long and unkempt and to adopt suitably romantic attitudes, taking their cue from old pictures of monks at prayer or seated beside a suitable still life of crucifix, skull and ancient Bible. Often such hermits were actually forbidden to speak to the company lest they should destroy the strange magic of the fiction.

One of the most extravagant of all follies was Ligori's recreation, in miniature, of Rome, at the Villa d'Este in Tivoli. As a favoured attraction for the English "travelling boys" and

ABOVE LEFT *A general view of the museum-like room in Brussels in which Thierry Bosquet displays the collection of exquisite miniature rooms he has created. Each is carefully scaled and meticulously finished down to the last detail.*

ABOVE RIGHT *A close-up view of a corner of the music salon reveals the precision with which even the smallest details have been realized. A carved and painted harpsichord, music stands and other instruments stand on a tiny reproduction of a Savonnerie carpet.*

others making their grand tour, it must have been a source not only of pleasure but also of envy. Indeed, envy and the consequent desire to emulate seems to have been a guiding force in the creation of many temples, grottoes and other follies. A good number are small-scale copies of celebrated buildings, while others make easily read allusions to particular styles or details. A late example, the Observatory at Worle in Wessex, was tricked out with an onion dome in direct emulation of the cheeky minarets and "wanton cupolae" – of the Royal Pavilion at Brighton. Just as the dividing lines between admiration and envy are often blurred, so too does the desire to emulate often blend imperceptibly, but nonetheless inexorably, into the need to equal and the mania to outdo. A case in point is Hadlow Castle in Kent, known locally – and with good reason – as May's Folly. Erected between 1838 and 1848 by George Ledwell Turner for Walter Barton May, the principal reason for the existence of such a vast, spindly Gothic tower seems to have been this eccentric squire's obsessive desire to rival that other extravagant builder, William Beckford. Could he have known of those insanely competitive Florentine families who vied with each other to erect the towers of San Gimignano? Though reaching the same impossibly vertiginous height, May's tower never came close to equalling the splendour and richness of Beckford's Fonthill Abbey. However, since Beckford's tower had, within a matter of only twenty years, sensationally collapsed into its own inadequate foundations, bringing down all but one tiny wing of the great edifice, May had the ultimate satisfaction of seeing his folly stand proud; it still does, even to this day, against all the odds and in defiance of every rule of sensible architectural practice.

On the most lavish imaginable scale of envious rivalry, poor, mad Ludwig II of Bavaria conceived the notion that he could emulate and outdo all the greatest royal castle and palace builders of Europe. Neuschwanstein, his pinnacled and battlemented Wagnerian dream of a Gothic, stronghold begun in 1869, remains his most famous creation, but it is at Linderhof, begun in 1870, the white neo-baroque palace perched high in the mountains but surrounded by improbable gardens with cascades and palm trees, that we first sense Ludwig's tragic delusion that he was a new Sun King, measuring himself against the might of Louis XIV.

At Hierenchiemsee, Ludwig's third great palace, begun in 1878 and built on an island in a lake, Ludwig made his most extraordinary bid to equal the glory of Versailles, creating a new Galerie des Glaces (Hall of Mirrors), even larger than the real thing. During his strange and theatrical reign, it was said that Ludwig dissipated between half and three-quarters of the entire wealth of the Bavarian state upon his schemes. In the end, after first withdrawing from society almost completely, he was impeached and imprisoned by his ministers, and declared insane by doctors in 1886. He escaped captivity one night, only to drown in somewhat suspicious circumstances in a moonlit mountain lake.

LEFT *Another of Thierry Bosquet's miniature masterpieces reproduces to scale the carved and gilded opulence of an early eighteenth-century theatre with its private boxes and grand throne beneath a baldachin.*

LEFT *In the Parisian apartment of Remy le Fur, a plaster cast of a colossal classical head forms the centrepiece of a group of sculptures ranging from primitive African carvings to the most refined of French eighteenth-century busts.*

FAR LEFT *Arranged like objects in a private museum, imposing scale and visual quirkiness are the uniting characteristics of the otherwise extremely diverse pieces that form the collection of Christophe Decarpentrie in Brussels.*

LEFT *Replete with carved and gilded ornamentation and highly coloured trompe l'oeil murals, Brian Lewis' London drawing room defies the more usual subdued, near monochromatic conventions of polite neoclassicism, seeming rather to evoke the bold and at times theatrical opulence of Roman decorative schemes.*

LEFT *In Brian Lewis'*
London drawing room,
an extensive landscape and
architectural capriccio fills
an entire wall and is
complemented by a trompe
l'oeil ceiling representing
a cloudy sky with groups
of flying putti and a floor
of painted flagstones.

ABOVE *A barbaric modern*
sofa and a contemporary
chandelier of twig-like
form prevent the drawing
room in Brian Lewis'
London home from
becoming simply an
historical pastiche.

FOLLOWING PAGE *Within a*
sculpture in the Tarot
Garden in Tuscany, Niki
de Saint Phalle has created
a bathroom lined with
concrete and mirror mosaic
and a shower compartment
that is encircled by a vast
sculptural snake.

The archetype of those driven to their own destruction by envy is the legendary Assyrian King Nimrud, who, jealous of divine power, sought to build a great tower to conquer the heavens. As Lord de Tabley tells the tale in his *Poems Dramatic and Lyrical* of 1893:

And the tower rose: the masons at its height
Could see the ocean now that we had left a year behind us…
And still they built: and mad in our desire
We waited; slowly height on height it drew:
"An hour and we attain it." Sudden light
Brake from above, "Ye armies, heaven is won:
I lead you, come." A roar behind me came,
As if against the land I led the sea:
And now I set my foot upon the stair –
When darkness drave upon my brain – I fell.

As Max Beerbohm put it, with his customary epigraphic precision: "the dullard's envy of brilliant men is always assuaged by the suspicion that they will come to a bad end."

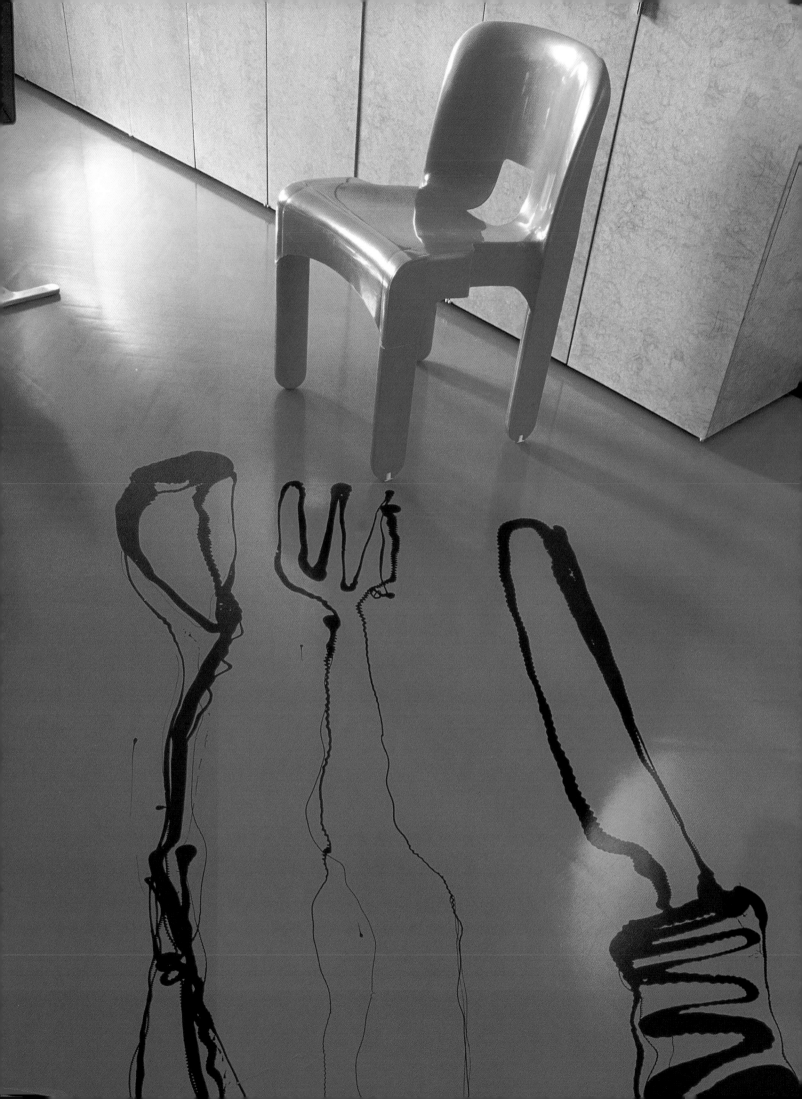

Gluttony

There is perhaps no better arena for the display of bizarre and recherché taste than the dining table. Caligula dined off flamingoes and the black flesh of peacocks, and held golden feasts. Nero's dining rooms had ceilings of fretted ivory, which would slide back to allow flowers to shower down upon his guests. This sheer, glorious ostentation has yet to be surpassed. Yet for the modern decadent sensibility, gluttony is refined to subtler epicurean pleasures: the jaded appetite craves smoked and spiced dishes, rare delicacies, strong and scented liquors.

Of literary evocations of decadent dining, perhaps the most extravagant is that described in Huysmans' novel *A Rebours.* The Duc Jean Floressas des Esseintes, mourning the temporary loss of his virility, holds a black feast: "Dining off black-bordered plates, the company had enjoyed turtle soup, Russian rye bread, ripe olives from Turkey, caviare, mullet botargo, black puddings from Frankfurt, game served in sauces the colour of liquorice and boot-polish, truffle jellies, chocolate creams, plum-puddings, nectarines, pears in grape-juice syrup, mulberries and black heart cherries. From dark-tinted glasses they had drunk the wines of Limagne and Roussillon, of Tenedos, Valdepeñas and Oporto. And after coffee and walnut cordial, they had rounded off the evening with kvass, porter and stout."

This feast illustrates one of the most delightful paradoxes of decadence, that style seems, so often, to take precedence over substance; here the sumptuousness of the array to be savoured is tempered and chastened by its funereal hue. Yet for Huysmans, as for the

PREVIOUS PAGES *Philippe Model's kitchen in Paris is arranged as a fantasy evocation of life in a château in the French countryside. An immense and disorganized* batterie de cuisine *is scattered about the room, while bowls, trays and trugs groan beneath an array of fruit and vegetables.*

LEFT *Thierry Bosquet's miniature country kitchen reproduces everything from table and kitchen utensils, such as a nutmeg grater, down to the oven and a tray of newly baked bread.*

ABOVE *The recreation of the basement kitchen in Dennis Severs' early eighteenth-century house in London's Spitalfields was based on the illustrations in Beatrix Potter's classic tale for children* The Tailor of Gloucester.

decadent reader who approaches the extravagances of des Esseintes in the right vein of seriousness and frivolity, the *vanitas* and *memento mori* imagery only add to the delectation; these delicious symbols of death provoke a frisson of subtly comingled horror and delight as they are consumed.

Yet a true *fête macabre* would not be black but scarlet. In a deep red profusion of *sang-de-bœuf* dishes would be bortsch, an array of rare and bloody meats, delicate sorbets of redcurrant and purple granadilla, dishes heaped with glistening and ruby-fleshed pomegranate seeds with their curiously astringent scent and thick sweet juice, bleeding velvet raspberries and sweets stained with the powerful essence of cochineal; to drink, the great deep crimson wines of Lafite and Margaux.

Just as black is the colour of mourning and of death, white is the cast of fear. Ghosts, faces white with terror, the plumage of predatory birds, the flesh of the deadly fungi Death Cap and Destroying Angel. A white feast, the table decorated with pallid sugar sculptures modelled on funerary monuments, illuminated by dim light from pewter candelabra, lilies and waxen magnolia exuding their heavy scent, would surely include white truffles, pale asparagus, sole Véronique, pellucid whitecurrants, soft fleshy Brillat-Savarin – undoubtedly the aesthete's cheese *par excellence* – and the nectareous wine Château d'Yquem, its flavour the result of the mould allowed to form on the grapes, the very essence of *pourriture noble*.

Although greenness is more habitually associated with qualities estranged from the decadent, health and vitality, these jarring connotations happily fade when we consider drinks. There is the strong cloying sweetness of green chartreuse; there is green tea, which in Sheridan le Fanu's story *Green Tea* (1872) serves as solace and stimulant for the solitary writer, yet which evokes the horrible apparition of a monkey with glowing eyes. Absinthe, the green goddess, the *sine qua non* of the decadent condition, with its lurid and unnatural viridescent glow, turning milky and glaucous with the addition of water, invokes visions both wonderful and terrible. Ernest Dowson, most wrecked of the 1890 poets of the "tragic generation," in *Absinthia Taetra*, captured precisely the strange sensations caused by the devastating wormwood:

Green changed to white, emerald to an opal: nothing was changed.
The man let the water trickle gently into his glass and as the green clouded, a mist fell away from his mind.
Then he drank opaline.

Memories and terrors beset him. The past tore after him like a panther and through the blackness of the present he saw the luminous tiger eyes of the things to be.
But he drank opaline.
…
The man had known the obscure night of the soul, and lay even now in the valley of humiliation; and the tiger menace of the things to be was red in the skies. But for a little while he had forgotten.
Green changed to white, emerald to an opal: nothing was changed.

PREVIOUS PAGES *In keeping with the Edwardian flavour of the rest of her house, Virginia Bates' dining room has a table laden with elegant glasses, pretty coloured decanters and exotic flowers beneath a sparkling chandelier.*

LEFT *Tony Duquette delighted in creating exotic places to dine all over his extensive house in the Hollywood Hills. In an intimate chinoiserie corner with a window overlooking lush gardens and beneath a mirrored ceiling, he groups Indian tooled silver chairs around a small table.*

ABOVE *The characteristically eclectic Duquette table setting includes abalone shell dishes on old Oriental famille rose plates, silver animals and crystals, all laid out upon a malachite-patterned cloth.*

"What is there in absinthe that makes it a separate cult?" mused Aleister Crowley (1875–1947), occultist, poet and *soi-disant* mage, in *Absinthe: the Green Goddess*: "The effects of its abuse are totally distinct from those of other stimulants. Even in ruin and in degradation it remains a thing apart: its victims wear a ghastly aureole all their own, and in their peculiar hell yet gloat with a sinister perversion of pride that they are not as other men."

Green is also reminiscent of corruption; the decadent craves gamey, over-ripe flavours, is a connoisseur of subtle degrees of decay. Salmon, buried in the earth with salt, sugar and dill, when resurrected, has become gravadlax; hung game, pungent and strong, acquires the soft texture of delicate suede; ripe cheese, fretted with spreading hyacinthine veins, acquires a harsh, sweet, almost ammoniacal savour. At the very pinnacle of deliquescence is the durian, bizarrest of fruits, with its appalling stench of putrefaction yet sweetest of flesh.

The heroine of Christina Rossetti's 1862 poem *Goblin Market* discovers the quasi-sexual experience inherent in eating as she gorges greedily on luscious, poisonous fruits:

She sucked and sucked and sucked the more
Fruits which that unknown orchard bore;
She sucked until her lips were sore.

For the jaded roué wishing to be reminded of the pleasures of the bedchamber, *bonnes bouches* may be savoured in the forms of European cakes and sweet pastries such as nipples of Venus, virgins' breasts and lady's thighs; the covert implications of cannibalism adding, perhaps, the final garnish of a lascivious *frisson* to the voluptuary's enjoyment.

Over the centuries, food has been the subject of extraordinary excess in terms of presentation and display. From the time of Trimalchio's feast celebrated in the lurid pages of the *Satyricon* of the late Roman poet Petronius, hosts and their guests have delighted in sheer pomp and the employment of the most artful contrivances to turn the eating of a meal into pure theatre. In the grandest houses, vast arrays of costly dishes, silver and gilded vessels and rare glasswares were piled up upon the credenza as a testament of wealth and magnificence, while the food itself was not just tastefully and temptingly arranged, but artificially coloured and often sculpted into fantastic forms. Too enervated to do anything but admire the table decoration, the true decadent loves the exquisite and elaborate shapes of these delicate, fleeting, fanciful structures and cares nothing for dreary nutritional value on a plate.

By the Middle Ages, Chaucer's Parson is horrified by what he finds defacing English tables, the "excess of diverse metes and drynkes, and namely swich manere bake-metes and dissh-metes, brennynge of wilde fir and peynted and castelled with papir, and semblable wast, so that it is abusioun for to thynke." Such disapproval is as salt to the decadent dinner table, intensifying flavour; without it our pleasures should be bland indeed.

A recurrent theme in the history of dining is the vast number of dishes served at the great feasts of antiquity or the lavish banquets of the eighteenth and early nineteenth centuries. Of the 140 dishes carried in by an army of servants at a dinner given by George IV at the Royal Pavilion in Brighton, it is unlikely that each guest tasted from more than a handful of them. For those who sat at the great long table glittering with silver-gilt and crystal, all that mattered was the unbelievable opulence of the palace, the profusion of delicacies, and the

RIGHT *One room in Dennis Severs' house was arranged to reflect the hard times of the nineteenth century in Spitalfields; at that time mussels and oysters, coarse bread and bottled beer were the staple fare of London's poor.*

FOLLOWING PAGE LEFT
The dining room of Brian Lewis' London house, with its stencilled walls and vast painted zodiacal roundel on the floor, is a homage to the bold neo-medieval style of William Burges' celebrated interiors, of the mid-1870s, for the Marquess of Bute at Cardiff Castle and Castell Coch.

FOLLOWING PAGE RIGHT
A close-up of Brain Lewis' dining room shows the painted dining table that hangs on chains from the mosaic ceiling. It has a raised section for the display of a centrepiece.

hospitality and convivial charm of Prinny himself, that plump and dandified voluptuary who occupied a vast chair – half as wide again as all the rest – at the head of the table.

The very greatest chef of the Regency years, Antonin Carême, was celebrated for his sculptural table centrepieces, or *pièces montées*, made from pastry, fruit and spun sugar. These architectural follies were constructed with fantastic intricacy: castles, ruins, grottoes, temples, galleons, birds and animals rose mountainously from dinner tables, surrounded by no less fabulous archipelagoes of brimming dishes, arranged with virtuoso skill and delicacy.

The decadent nostalgically seeks to recreate the lost eras of splendid artistry. The monochromatic feasts begun in Roman times are refined to the subtlest shades, ever more bizarre combinations of flavours are sought, ever more exquisite delicacies. Yet the decadent's constitution is weak, and soon epicurism will be a memory of more vigorous times, the fondest remembrance of gastronomic passion recalled in the most exquisite tranquillity.

Wrath

It was said of the hyper-sensitive aesthete Charles Ricketts that at his beautiful house, full of precious things, "one false note could be an outrage." Huysmans' neurasthenic hero orders his servants to wear felt slippers so that he need never endure the sound of footsteps. The narrator of Poe's Ligeia, sequestered in his tapestried turret, mourning his lost love, comes to loathe his unpoetic second wife "with a hatred belonging more to demon than to man", a sentiment echoed in his weird visions conjured by the ghastly decoration. To the highly strung mind, morbidly sensitive to vulgarity, anything but the most exquisite causes irritation beyond endurance.

*P*erhaps the most extreme manifestation of a debased and decadent mind is found in the impulse to transform arms into decoration, to demonstrate capacity for violence and brutality through aesthetic display. Armouries, which boast great trophies of weapons, often highly wrought, inlaid with silver or gold and elaborately engraved, are the site of this uncomfortable union of decoration and battle. These martial arrays of swords, spears, clubs, pikes and guns inevitably invite as their backdrop blood red walls, a colour which brings vividly to mind the use and past history of the gleaming blades, and which also, according to colour theory, stimulates the nerves, provoking agitation and choler. Such elegant yet powerful displays suggest that in the owner, ferocity and urbanity are held in fragile equilibrium.

This delight in exquisitely wrought weaponry is to be found in many castles and palaces. In England one of the most spectacular examples is the Guard Chamber, the first of the great seventeenth-century ceremonial enfilade of state rooms in Hampton Court, in which William III's gunsmith, a man named Harris, arranged all over the oak panelling more than 3000 pieces with an obsessive eye for geometry. Another of the greatest of these arrays of arms and armour can still be seen in its original setting in the Palazzo Ducale in Venice, where it forms a fitting testament to the subtle ruthlessness and highly developed aestheticism of the city's rulers in the great days of the Republic's power. In more recent times, Cecil Beaton also created a series of famous images in this idiom when during World War II he photographed the wrecked remains of a burnt-out tank in the desert, having had soldiers pull the twisted metal remains into compositions of strange, modernist beauty.

The other, darker side of this coin is the decoration of places of incarceration, where architecture and decoration combine to inspire fear and dread. In Venice's Palazzo Ducale,

PREVIOUS PAGES *Juxtaposed with a sleek modern bed of brown leather in a minimal interior in Paris by decorator Oddes, a nineteenth-century horn trophy chair seems to take on an aggressive stance, like a zoo animal caged in an alien environment.*

LEFT *A panache of African horns creates a curious art nouveau pattern of repeating sinuous curves in a St Tropez conservatory owned by the hairdresser Alexandre.*

ABOVE *Faux leopard- and zebra-skin upholstery adds to the sense of danger engendered by an array of pieces of trophy furniture in Alexandre's St Tropez conservatory. Although the exotic hothouse plants belong more to the jungle than the savannahs, their spiky qualities continue the edgy theme.*

in the sixteenth and seventeenth centuries, the Sala della Bussola was the antechamber of the much-feared Council of Ten, elected governors who privately investigated and punished all state crimes, and had a reputation for violence and mystery. Here, through the infamous Bocca di Leone, secret denunciations were handed in. Next to the palace, with its gorgeous paintings and splendid state rooms, stands the gaunt prison with its labyrinthine series of tomblike cells, sometimes utterly dark, sometimes oppressive and suffocating, often flooded: the Pozzi, the Camerotti and the Piombi.

Prisons were never more vividly or nightmarishly imagined than by the eighteenth-century Venetian artist Giovanni Battista Piranesi in his horrifying *Carceri* series of etchings conceived in the mid-1740s. In these designs Piranesi conjured dim, cavernous spaces of staggering architectural complexity. Narrow staircases, which cling to and wind precipitously up vast, vertiginous walls, seemingly lead nowhere; galleries and arches multiply in bewildering confusion; chains, gallows, spikes, nooses and indistinct instruments of torture provide decorative relief and seem to grow organically from the darkest corners of these comfortless places. The unfortunate inhabitants are dwarfed by the restless structures of these infernal temples to punishment and incarceration. Indeed, Piranesi's famous images of Roman architecture are reminders of the cruelty of ancient Rome, in particular the Colosseum, that theatre where from the comfort of his marble apartment the emperor would watch as gladiators fought to the death, or men were devoured by wild beasts.

PREVIOUS PAGES *In the Nympheum Omega chapel next to his villa in Vienna, Ernst Fuchs's ranks of sculpted wing-forms frame the view of a warlike triple-headed deity flanked by two flaming masks. Seen against a background of stained glass depicting a troubled firmament, this bizarre ensemble is invested with a weird visual power.*

LEFT *An old crystal-handled steel knife plunged into what seems to be the wreck of a once grand chandelier forms an unsettling still life, the creation of American antique dealer Michael Trapp.*

ABOVE *Christophe Vachère of Brussels is another collector fascinated by the macabre. One among his many treasures is this chilling silver skull.*

Piranesi's designs leave an indelible mark on the imaginations of all who dwell on their horrifying structures. William Beckford, while travelling in Venice in 1780, recorded his sensations on passing underneath the Bridge of Sighs, which leads to the sinister depths of the Ducal prisons:

> I shuddered whilst passing below; and believe it is not without cause, this structure is named Ponte dei Sospiri. Horrors and dismal prospects haunted my fancy on my return. I could not dine in peace, so strongly was my imagination affected; but snatching my pencil, I drew chasms and subterraneous hollows, the domain of fear and torture, with chains, racks, wheels and dreadful engines in the style of Piranesi.

Although Piranesi's own creations were, for the most part, an architecture of the imagination, his influence on the work of his contemporaries was considerable and many buildings bore the unmistakable stamp of his extraordinary vision. Soon after the publication of later editions of the *Carceri* etchings, printed in the 1760s and well known to English connoisseurs, the prolific young architect George Dance, who had actually met Piranesi in Rome, designed the new Newgate Prison in 1769. One of the most dramatic architectural conceptions of its age, the prison presented a visual dramatization of its function – the massive, windowless walls of huge blackened stone blocks created an aura of menace and oppression. Over forbidding doorways hung heavy swags of chains and manacles, decorative elements as macabre as they were capricious. Because of its central location in the city and its chilling, theatrical presence, Newgate became deeply impressed upon the national consciousness, its very name enshrined in the popular phrase "as black as Newgate's knocker."

Gothic novels of the late eighteenth century take up the story of fearsome architecture and decoration. Horace Walpole in *The Castle of Otranto* of 1765, and followers such as Beckford and Mrs Radcliffe, use haunted castles and ruins in order to evoke a sense of dread through the antiquity of the rooms and their native malefic spectres. Sir Walter Scott wrote in 1827 of *The Tapestried Chamber* with its gloomy and antique air, from which emanated a baneful and terrifying spectre. This association of architecture and decoration with malign presences was taken up again later in the nineteenth century with the rise of the horror story. The American author Edgar Allan Poe, who himself wrote an essay on decoration, invests houses, rooms and furnishings with a kind of seething, visceral life, either as grotesque manifestations of the narrator's emotions, or as devices used to torment the inhabitant. The narrator of his 1843 short story *The Pit and the Pendulum*, a prisoner of the Inquisition, seems to be incarcerated in one of Piranesi's more terrifying dungeons, in complete blackness, his nerves unstrung by his sightless groping for the shape of his room. When a sulphurous light makes his cell dimly visible, he sees that it is "rudely daubed in all the hideous and repulsive devices to which the charnel superstition of the monks has given rise," and that the very walls, ceiling and floor themselves have been fashioned as instruments of torture. Later in the century Bram Stoker and Sheridan Le Fanu invested ordinary domestic interiors with the supernatural wrath of their previous inhabitants. More recently, film makers have developed stock images of malevolent architecture, such as haunted houses and castles, either dark and turreted

PREVIOUS PAGES *In a bedroom in Franca and Carla Sozzani's Marrakech house, the glow from the deep cranberry-coloured glass in the small iron-grilled window falling upon vast crimson counterpanes gives the room an air of menace, as though it were prepared for some sinister ritual.*

RIGHT *An unsettling atmosphere pervades this Parisian bedchamber designed by Gaetano Pesce; the weird, ruched bedcover that appears to be bound by heavy ropes suggests the setting of one of Edgar Allen Poe's macabre tales.*

FOLLOWING PAGES *A pair of massive French wrought-iron grilles form a suitable dramatic entrance to a Trois Garçons' room filled with 1970s furniture. Pieces from an era usually considered lightweight and frothy seem to take on a more sinister character.*

RIGHT *In an interior created by the painter Pierre Peyrol, the use of reflective flooring and a ceiling with endlessly repeating mirror coffering has a profoundly unsettling effect. The use of silvered, shell-backed grotto-chairs and other decorative pieces enhances the slight sense of disorientation.*

FAR RIGHT *In an apartment in New York for Ruth Schuman, the designer Gaetano Pesce places great emphasis on the use of bold graphic effects on the floor. Hugely overscaled and aggressive caricature faces automatically command the attention of the viewer.*

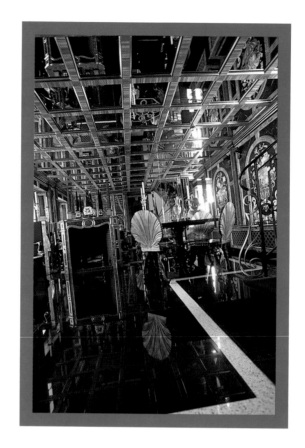

with twisting staircases, and secret rooms, epitomised by that in Jack Clayton's 1961 film *The Innocents,* or the towering, gloomy Victorian structures of Norman Bates' house in *Psycho* and the empty Colorado hotel of Stanley Kubrick's *The Shining.*

This filmic vocabulary of horror has been adopted by fair-grounds, where the ghost train houses the quintessence of decoration intended to frighten and thrill; yet often, out of the darkness the images and effigies that flash by are not of ghosts but scenes of torture and execution, and the ride becomes like a nightmare journey through a dank gaol. Similarly, Madame Tussaud's Chamber of Horrors, and its imitators, seem to exert a perennial fascination for this sort of theatrical taming of the true horror of human cruelty. On a more exalted, and perhaps psychologically more disturbing level, in Huysmans' *A Rebours,* the anti-hero, des Esseintes, devotes one room of his house to a series of ebony-framed prints by the Dutch engraver Jan Luyken. Around the bright red tapestried walls of his boudoir hangs Luyken's ferocious studies in wrath and cruelty, his *Religious Persecutions.* These pictures, relates Huysmans, "full of abominable fancies, reeking of burnt flesh, dripping with blood, echoing with screams and curses, made des Esseintes' flesh creep whenever he went into the red boudoir, and he remained rooted to the spot, choking with horror."

It is curious and perhaps subtly indicative of the deep decadence of our unsettled era that even the most powerful images or descriptions of wrath, horror and inhumanity seem all too often to be tinged with the camp reactions of the fetishist or the cool depravity of the Marquis de Sade. But the crowd has always loved the theatre of cruelty whether in the form of the display of traitors' heads on spikes and public executions of past ages, or of the Japanese endurance gameshows watched by millions on television today.

LEFT *This stuffed bulldog,
adorned with a jewelled
head-dress and wings by
the Trois Garçons, has the
appearance of a nightmare
creature from the late
eighteenth-century paintings
of Henry Fuseli or one of the
Victorian fairy painters
such as Dadd or Fitzgerald.*

ABOVE *Unlike their
aggressive bulldog, the
Trois Garçons' stuffed
leopard dressed up in a
1920s diamante head-dress
seems strangely cowed and
diminished in power.*

FOLLOWING PAGES *In the
Brussels home of collector
Christophe Decarpentrie
an 1840s paper-knife
embellished with a sinister
figure of Mephistopheles
lies on a volume of the
works of Montfaucon,
the early eighteenth-century
scholar of antiquities,
which is open at a page
illustrating mysterious
ancient deities.*

ffent pas.
planche suiva
& les mains
z far les ori
ecretiale de fo
ais quel
bien quel
qui leur

raute
la des cho
, dit-on, cinqu
s volontiers qu'il y a e
he, qui raconte la même chofe,
xercices des athletes; c'étoit à peu
it rond & plat, on le faifoit de
là gagnoit, qui le jettoit ou plus
que l'on appelle en grec παγκράτιον &
ueurs en tous ces jeux s'appelloient
Il y en a pourtant qui diftinguent

pugilatu qui victus fuerat herbam adverfario fuo
porrigebat, qua re fe victum illumque victorem
declarabat.
VIII. Athletæ illi faltibus etiam fefe exerce-
bant, qui faltu longius fpatium tranfiliebat, victor
cenfebatur. Qua de re quædam leguntur, quibus
fides habeatur. Memoratur quidam Phayllus
des quinquaginta fex uno faltu prætergreffus
quod utique tam infolens effe videtur
rorem in numero a Tzetze prolato f
Euftathius qui rem narrat, cumdem ipfum nume-
rum haberet.
Difci ludus athletarum item exercitium erat. Dif-
cus hodiernæ noftro fimilis fuiffe videtur; fecundus
ba , ex lapide fiebat , aut ex ferro
ficut atque planos ,ex lapide fiebat , aut ex ferro
ille victor aut qui altior aut qui
habentes convenerat.

Sloth

"Ah, why should life all labour be?" sang Tennyson's Lotos-Eaters, "give us long rest or death, dark death, or dreamful ease." These marooned mariners were content with beds of amaranth and moly, yet a more luxurious retreat in which to indulge languid reverie and sybaritic pleasure is sought by the modern decadent. Hung with rich silks and tapestries, draped with sumptuous Fortuny velvets and gleaming furs, the dim chamber offers respite to the jaded and the exhausted; the shifting arabesque patterns of the smoke of incense and Turkish cigarettes please the eye and provoke bizarre visions.

For thousands of years, quietness and calm, meditation and the contemplation of beauty, have been valued in the cultures of the East as the very highest aims and attainments of life; in the West, by stark contrast, we seem always to have celebrated bustle, tiresome activity and even aggression. We mistrust the quiet and the contemplative. We have actually demonized sloth, and, in the North, home of the dreary Protestant work ethic, we have even come to despise the Mediterranean peoples for their civilized hour of languor in the heat of the day at siesta time. It has been left to the happy few, to the decadents, aesthetes and dreamers, to savour the precious delights of inactivity and to indulge in the – preferably gentle – pursuit of beauty.

There is a terrible irony in the fact that "progress," for so long the great aim of the *soi-disant* civilized world, has rarely led to greater contentment. The eighteenth century was probably the last moment in which most places were quiet; since that time the pursuit of progress and the relentless destruction of peace have gone hand in hand. During the late nineteenth century ordinary life became ever faster and more exhausting; burgeoning cities and rampant commercialism, more and more rapid trains, the new-fangled motor cars, the telegraph and telephones all contributed to an increased strain on the nerves. At this time, even in the everyday world, specific new dangers began to be diagnosed in the ostensible "benefits" of progress: "railway spine" was believed to be a disorder of the nervous system caused by the effects on the spinal cord of the cruel jolts and unendurable vibrations of fast train travel. Everywhere, inexorably, noise and frenetic urban bustle invaded and destroyed old-fashioned quietness and calm; on every hand, the old virtues of repose and contemplation were swept away by a seemingly universal obsession with novelty and speed. By the turn of the century the once vague, age-old, millennial sense of disquiet was accorded a new status as a medical condition

PREVIOUS PAGE *With typical humour, Brizio Bruschi arranges a nineteenth-century alabaster figure of an outrageously decadent, reclining fairy on a fur rug next to a luxurious shell-headed daybed.*

LEFT *In a penthouse apartment in New York, David Roos, the master of luxurious upholstery, arranges the most decadently sybaritic take on the classic three-piece suite.*

RIGHT *Franca and Carla Sozzani's luxuriously appointed bathroom in Marrakech invites the most luxurious languor. With its vast ceiling height and sumptuous fittings it seems worlds apart from its standard European, utilitarian counterpart.*

PREVIOUS PAGES *In her London house, Sera Hersham-Loftus arranges a wittily seductive corner, juxtaposing a daybed covered with an old Aubusson rug and piled high with cushions with a photograph originally used as an advert created by Barbara Hulanicki for her celebrated 1960s store, Biba.*

LEFT *In a bathroom in the Marrakech house of Franca and Carla Sozzani, traditional pierced metal star-shaped lanterns shed an intriguing glow upon a room screened by shimmering silken curtains. A mosaic tiled bath of suitable scale for two – or more – invites the most languorous of bathing.*

ABOVE *Sera Hersham-Loftus has created a bathroom to linger in, in a chapel-like space under the roof of her London house, installing a superb early nineteenth-century French metal bath of sarcophagus form.*

and given a new, Germanic name, "angst," while, by a bizarre twist, the old sin of sloth came to be defined as a pathological state, popularly held to be the result of enervation, a feebleness engendered of degeneracy and decay.

In the face of this idiot whirlwind of modernity, some sensitive beings, feeling their nerves tautened and twisted to breaking point, gave way to good old-fashioned sloth, to ennui and to newer and ever-subtler psychological maladies. Neurasthenia, that nervous state resulting from the constant anxiety and exhaustion brought on by the modern mania for innovation and activity, came to be seen as the quintessential affliction of the new decadent, aesthetic soul. In Huysmans' novel *A Rebours*, des Esseintes, the type of all neurasthenic dandies, finds the only solution to the problem, and the only possible escape from the hideous onrush of the present, in complete withdrawal from society and quotidian existence into a world of utterly rarefied, aesthetic sloth. Only in his exquisitely decorated château, untroubled by any activity and surrounded by wonderful pictures and precious things, can the extraordinary aristocrat cultivate his obscure desires and hone his febrile senses to perfection.

Thus, the finest and most decadent aesthetic spirits of the Victorian era shunned the horrors of modernity and cherished the ideal of sloth as the perfection of artificial existence. Extolling it as the ultimate of intellectual states, they explored all the subtle charms of "*luxe, calme et volupté.*" Charles Baudelaire and his circle of fellow Romantic writers and decadents, who called themselves "Le Club des Haschischins," sought to create an opiate heaven in their notorious sessions held in the ancient Parisian palace the Hôtel de Lauzun. In England, Dante Gabriel Rossetti, Pre-Raphaelite and foremost of the symbolist poets and painters, all but shut himself away in his old, dark house in Cheyne Walk at the heart of bohemian Chelsea. There he worked on an endless, curiously repetitive series of

PREVIOUS PAGES *The ideal of the bedroom as a personal haven has great appeal. Filled with a selection of choice objects and with books and other diversions to hand, Ramuntcho de Saint Armand's distinctive red bedroom in his Normandy house fulfils every expectation.*

LEFT *The Arab notion of furnishings, based on rugs, divans and cushions, carries seductive connotations of indolence for Europeans more used to hard, high furniture. In New York, the house of artist Izhar Patkin groups sumptuous embroidered cushions, low seats and a heavily tooled Moroccan pouffe around a low Damascus brass coffee table, lit by a lamp designed by the owner.*

RIGHT *An accomplished stylist, in one corner of her grand London flat, Nathalie Hambro has created a visually appealing group of highly disparate objects centred on a superb and rare nineteenth-century cast-iron daybed.*

PREVIOUS PAGES *In the main bedroom of Franca and Carla Sozzani's Moroccan house, four tall casement windows are shaded by paisley shawls. Soft pink walls, huge traditional lanterns, thick cyclamen pink local rugs, a bed designed by Kris Ruhs and a profusion of cushions create a sense of decadent luxury.*

LEFT *In a New York apartment of rich hues and vibrant patterns, the artist Dianne Blell's blue Persian cat has a miniature bed of its own, thereby striking a note that is at once supremely indolent and gently amusing.*

ABOVE *Throughout the centuries, and in all cultures, rich fabrics have been a touchstone of wealth and a seductive invitation to luxury and self-indulgence. Franca and Carla Sozzani mix delicious fabrics, old and new, from India and Turkey as well as local sources.*

pictures of languidly sensual *femmes fatales*, but finally gave himself up to dreams inspired by the opium-derived drug chloral. Richard Le Gallienne, author of *The Romantic 90s* (1926), described Rossetti at this time, saying that he "dwelt in mysterious sacrosanct seclusion like some high priest behind the veil . . ."

A little later, the dandies of the *fin-de-siècle*, dedicated *flâneurs* like their counterparts in the early decades of the nineteenth century, proudly proclaimed their lack of any occupation as a badge of honour and insisted upon the all-absorbing importance of the pose of idle elegance. Theirs was a world, an existence, that exuded, in the words of Carl Hahn, early twentieth-century literary critic and editor, "a strong aroma of excess and ennui, available to those with the leisure and resources vigorously to pursue sensation." The aesthetes and connoisseurs of the day followed the injunction of the English critic and essayist Walter Pater to seek after beauty, to cherish "Art for Art's sake," and rejoiced in Oscar Wilde's bold dictum that, in the end, "all Art is quite useless."

Today, daunted by the overwhelming pressure to embrace progress, change and the manic pursuit of "success," we should do well to remember that other delightful aphorism of Wilde's: "Ambition is the last refuge of the failure." Now, it seems, sloth has an ever more important role to play as one of the only sure ways to hold the worst excesses of the modern world at bay, and in particular to counter its baleful concepts of "entertainment" and "leisure." For the dandy, the aesthete and the epicure, sloth is now, as never before, an essential attitude and perfect pose, allowing us to reach out across time to the nineties of Wilde, back to those more leisurely and spacious days of the eighteenth century, and thence to the seventeenth, the greatest era of sensual poetic introspection.

Andrew Marvell, whose poems *To His Coy Mistress* and *The Garden* were written in the 1650s, delighted in descriptions of slothful sensuality, declaring, as he thought of his coy mistress that:

> an hundred years should go to praise
> thine eyes, and on thy forhead gaze.
> two hundred to adore each breast;
> but thirty thousand to the rest.

In the same vein, in his sublime evocation of the delicious languor of an English garden, he wrote:

> What wondrous life is this I lead!
> Ripe apples drop about my head;
> The luscious clusters of the vine
> Upon my mouth do crush their wine;
> The nectarene, and curious peach,
> Into my hands themselves do reach;
> Stumbling on melons, as I pass,
> Ensnared with flowers, I fall on grass.

RIGHT *Architecturally one of the finest rooms in Franca and Carla Sozzani's Marrakech house, this sitting room seems less traditional and more like the interiors in Arabian Nights style invented by the great couturier Paul Poiret in those last languorous days before World War I.*

FAR RIGHT *Bill Willis is the doyen of decorators in Morocco and has done much to revive local materials and crafts. In his own home in Marrakech, a painstakingly restored traditional Arab house, he has gathered a rich mix of furnishings.*

The culmination of Marvell's poetic theme lay in the ultimate surrender of intellect to the delicious torpor of the afternoon; leaving only "a green thought in a green shade."

Curiously, it is a little difficult, today, to imagine real sloth – that is to say, the precious and exquisitely honed sloth of the decadents – in the open air. It is easy enough to laze in a garden; true sloth seems positively to require a perfect chamber. The exclusion of the boisterous outside world is essential; softness, dimness and rich stuffs, murmuring music and sweet fragrances seem to be the prerequisites of the decadent sanctuary. There have been many literary evocations of the veiled "within" and writers have delighted in describing the details of curtains and tapestries decorated with strange devices; lingering like connoisseurs over the differing qualities of luxurious fabrics, enumerating the softness and thickness of velvets or the dull sheen of ancient embroideries. None though, perhaps, has ever caught more precisely the feel of such chambers of the languid imagination as Edgar Allan Poe, with his weirdly unsettling description, in his essay *The Philosophy of Furniture* written in the 1840s, of a mournful, almost oppressive, crimson-draped, mirror-hung room, or in those particularly haunting lines from his 1845 poem *The Raven*:

And the silken, sad, uncertain rustling of each purple curtain
Thrilled me – filled me with fantastic terrors never felt before.

PREVIOUS PAGES *Rusty scaffolding poles support the shelving that houses a highly personal cabinet of curiosities formed by Vincent Darré in his Parisian apartment. Such disorganized yet utterly delectable assemblages only come together over a long period of random collecting.*

ABOVE *Philippe Model likes amusing touches in decoration, such as the painted stripes of more than fifty colours around this traditional panelled room. His daybed smothered in cushions seems to be another jeu d'esprit at the expense of serious period decoration.*

RIGHT *Lillian Williams' extraordinary collection of eighteenth- and early nineteenth-century shoes forms a curious and eloquent testament to the decadent spirit: an assemblage of the most exquisite and luxurious possessions of women who were seldom required to walk more than a short distance across rich carpets or manicured lawns.*

Directory

The Sequestered Decadent

Books:

A Gerits and Son
Antiquarian booksellers
Prinsengracht 445
1016 HN Amsterdam
The Netherlands
Tel: +31 020 627 2285
www.nvva.nl/gerits

Colin Page
Antiquarian booksellers
36 Duke Street
Brighton BN1 1AG
UK
Tel: +44 (0)1273 325 954

Heywood Hill
Booksellers
10 Curzon Street
London W1J 5HH
UK
Tel: +44 (0)20 7629 0647

Maggs Bros.
Antiquarian booksellers
50 Berkeley Square
London W1J 5BA
UK
Tel: +44 (0)20 7493 7160
www.maggs.com

Pictures and Prints:

Childs Gallery
169 Newbury Street
Boston
MA 02116
USA
Tel: +1 617 266 1108
email: info@childsgallery.com
www.childsgallery.com

Julian Hartnoll
14 Mason's Yard
London SW1Y 6BU,
UK
Tel: +44 (0)20 7839 3842

Peter Nahum
The Leicester Gallery
5 Ryder Street
London SW1Y 6PY
UK
Tel: +44 (0)20 7930 6059

Furniture and Antiques:

Chiavacci Antichita
Via della Spada 41-56-60/r
50100 Florence
Italy
Tel/fax: +39 055 239 8996

Christopher Gibbs
Paintings and decorative furniture
3 Dove Walk
London SW1W 8PH
UK
Tel: +44 (0)20 7730 8200

Clinton Howell Antiques
18 East Street 74th Street
New York
NY 10021
USA
Tel: +1 212 517 5879
email: clintonhowell@
mindspring.com
www.clintonhowell.com

David Gill
60 Fulham Road
London SW3 6HH
UK
Tel: +44 (0)20 7589 5946

Joss Graham Oriental Textiles
Textiles from the Middle and
Far East
10 Eccleston Street
London SW1W 9LT
UK
Tel: +44 (0)20 7730 4370

Mallett at Bourdon House
2 Davies Street
London W1K 3DW
UK
Tel: +44 (0)20 7629 2444
email: antiques@mallett.co.uk
www.mallett.co.uk

China, Glass and Cutlery:

Christopher Sheppard
Antique Glass
10 Richmond Mansions
248 Old Brompton Road
London SW5 9HL
UK
Tel: +44 (0)20 7373 9452
Fax: +44 (0)20 7341 9522

Thomas Goode and Co.
China, Glass, Silver and Antiques
19 South Audley Street
London W1K 2BN
UK
Tel: +44 (0)20 7499 2823

Bathroom Fittings:

Czech and Speake
125 Fulham Road
London SW3 6RT
UK
Tel: +44 (0)20 7225 3667

Fabrics:

V V Rouleaux
Ribbons, trimmings and braids
54 Sloane Street
London SW1W 8AX
UK
Tel: +44 (0)20 7730 3125

Stationery:

Frank Smythson
Diaries, stationery and
leather goods
40 Bond Street
London W1S 2DE
UK
Tel: +44 (0)20 7629 8558

Soolip Paperie and Press
8646 Melrose Avenue
Los Angeles
CA 90069
USA
Tel: +1 310 360 0545

Legatoria Polliero
Frari 2995
Venice
Italy
Tel: +39 041 85130

Flowers and Plants:

Clifton Nurseries Ltd.
Shop, greenhouse and
information
5a Clifton Villas
Little Venice
London W9 2PH
UK
Tel: +44 (0)20 7289 6851

Pulbrook and Gould
Florist
Liscartan House
127 Sloane Street
London SW1X 9AS
UK
Tel: +44 (0)20 7730 0030

Urban Gardener
1006 West Armitage Avenue
Chicago
IL 60614
USA
Tel: +1 773 477 2070
www.urbangardenerchicago.com

Wild at Heart
Florist
49a Ledbury Road
London W11 2AA
UK
Tel: +44 (0)20 7727 3095

Curiosities:

Deyrolle
Taxidermy, natural
history, geology
46 rue du Bac
75007 Paris
France
Tel: +33 1 42 22 3007

Shell World
41 Kings Road
Brighton BN1 1NA
UK
Tel: +44 (0)1273 327 664

Wildlife Artistry Taxidermy
Larry C Reese
215 Lands End Road
Centerville
MD 21617
USA
Tel: +1 410 758 2000

The Dandy

Hatters:

Anthony Peto
Chapelier
56 rue Tiquetonne
Paris 2
France
Tel: +33 1 40 26 60 68

James Lock and Co.
6 St. James' Street
London SW1A 1EF
UK
Tel: +44 (0)20 7930 5849
www.lockhatters.co.uk

Clothes:

All Our Yesterdays
Vintage clothes and accessories
Portsmouth
UK
Tel/fax: +44 (0)23 9286 3248

Davenport and Co.
Dee Davenport Howe
146 Bowdoin Street
Springfield
MA 01109,
USA
Tel +1 413 781 1505
email: dee@davenportandco.com
www.davenportandco.com

**Gallery of Antique Costume
and Textiles**
2 Church Street
Marylebone
London NW8 8ED
UK
Tel/fax: +44 (0)20 7723 9981
www.gact.co.uk

Linda Wrigglesworth
Dealer in antique Chinese
silk robes and textiles
34 Brook Street
London W1Y 1YA
UK
Tel: +44 (0)20 7408 0177

Steinberg and Tolkien
Vintage clothing
193 Kings Road
London SW3 5ED
UK
Tel: +44 (0)20 7376 3660

Stuart Craig
Antique clothing and accessories
Unit 72 Ground Floor
Admiral Vernon Antiques Arcade
141–149 Portobello Road
London W11 2DY
UK
Tel: +44 (0)20 7221 8662

Voyage
Women
115c Fulham Road
London SW3 6RL
UK
Tel: +44 (0)20 7823 9581
Men
175 Fulham Road
London SW3 6JW
UK
Tel: +44 (0)20 7352 8611

Shoes:
Emma Hope's Shoes
Delicate shoes
53 Sloane Square
London SW1W 8AX
UK
Tel: +44 (0)20 7259 9566

John Lobb
Bespoke bootmakers
9 St. James' Street
London SW1A 1EF
UK
Tel: +44 (0)20 7930 3664

Linda Campisano Millinery
900 North Michigan Avenue
Chicago
IL 60611
USA
Tel +1 312 337 1004
www.hatsalon.com

Tricorni
Calle del Lovo
San Marco 4813
Venice
Italy
Tel: +39 041 26454

Underwear:
Axfords
Corsetry
82 Centurion Road
Brighton BN1 3LN, UK
Tel: +44 (0)1273 327 944
email: michael@axfords.com
www.axfords.com

Clone Zone
Fetish wear
32 St. James' Street
Brighton
UK
Tel: +44 (0)1273 626 442

Rigby and Peller
Corsetry and lingerie
2 Hans Road
London SW3 1RX
UK
Tel: +44 (0)20 7589 9293
www.rigbyandpeller.com

Jewels:
Antiquarius
135 Kings Road
London SW3 4PW
UK
Tel: +44 (0)20 7351 5353

Edith Weber and Associates
Antique Jewelry
994 Madison Avenue
New York
NY 10021
USA
Tel/fax: +1 212 570 9668
email: info@antique-jewelry.com
www.antique-jewelry.com

Perfume and Toiletries:
Bourbon French Parfums
525 St. Ann Street
New Orleans
LA 70116
USA
Tel: +1 504 522 4480
email: info@neworleans
perfume.com
www.neworleansperfume.com

Penhaligons
Perfumiers
16–17 Burlington Arcade
London W1J OPW
UK
Tel: +44 (0)20 7629 1416
www.penhaligons.co.uk

Barbers:
Geo F Trumper
9 Curzon Street
London W1J 5HG
UK
Tel: +44 (0)20 7499 1850

Travel Goods:
Connolly Luxury Goods
Fine leather luggage
32 Grosvenor Crescent Mews
London SW1X 7EX
UK
Tel: +44 (0)20 7235 3883

The Epicurean

Food:
Camisa I and Co.
Italian Delicatessen
61 Old Compton Street
London W1D 6HS
UK
Tel: +44 (0)20 7437 7610

Debauve et Galais
Chocolatiers
30 rue des Saints Pères
Paris 7
France
Tel: +33 1 45 48 5467

Fauchon
The gourmet's delight
26 place de la Madeleine
Paris 8
France
Tel: +33 1 47 42 6011

Frank Godfrey
Free-range butcher
7 Highbury Park
London N5 1QJ
UK
Tel: +44 (0)20 7226 2425

Harrods Food Hall
Art Deco tiled halls
Knightsbridge
London SW1X 7XL
UK
Tel: +44 (0)20 7730 1234
www.harrods.com

Hester's Butchers
344 Kennington Lane
London SE11 5HY
UK
Tel: +44 (0)20 7735 9121
www.qmsdirectory.org.uk/
london/hesters.html

La Fromagerie
Delicatessen
30 Highbury Park
London N5 2AA
UK
Tel: +44 (0)20 7359 7440

La Maison de la Truffe
Perigodian specialities
19 place de la Madeleine
Paris 8
France
Tel: +33 1 42 66 1001

La Poisonnerie
Freshest Fish
Fisherman's Wharf
Brighton Road
Shoreham-by-Sea
Sussex BN43 6RE
UK
Tel: +44 (0)1273 463 014

Partridges of Sloane Street
Delicatessen
132 Sloane Street
London SW1X 9AT
UK
Tel: +44 (0)20 7730 0651

Paxton and Whitfield
Fine cheeses
93 Jermyn Street
London SW1Y 6JE
UK
Tel: +44 (0)20 7930 0259
www.cheesemongers.co.uk

Rogers' Chocolates Ltd
Head Office
913 Government Street
Victoria
BC V8W 1X5
Canada
Tel: +1 250 384 7021
Email: info@rogerschocolates.com
www.rogerschocolates.com

Spring's Smoked Salmon
Salmon curers
Edburton
West Sussex BN5 9LN
UK
Tel: +44 (0)1273 857 338

Drink:

Berry Bros. and Rudd
Wine merchant
3 St. James' Street
London SW1A 1EG
UK
Tel: +44 (0)20 7396 9600
email: customerservice@bbr.com
www.bbr.com

House of Glunz
1206 North Wells Street
Chicago
IL 60610
USA
Tel: +1 312 642 3000

Milroys of Soho Ltd.
Whisky merchant
3 Greek Street
London W1D 4NX
UK
Tel: +44 (0)20 7437 0893
email: Whiskey.London@
milroys.co.uk
www.milroys.co.uk

Places of Interest

London
Leighton House
12 Holland Park Road
London W14 8LZ
UK
Tel: +44 (0)20 7602 3316

Sir John Soane's Museum
13 Lincolns Inn Fields
London WC2A 3BP
UK
Tel: +44 (0)20 7430 0175

The Victoria and Albert Museum
Cromwell Road
South Kensington
London SW7 2RL
Tel: +44 (0)20 7942 2000
Fax +44 (0)20 7942 2266
www.vam.ac.uk

Paris
Gustave Moreau Museum
Gloomy, hieratic splendour
14 rue de la Rochfoucauld
Paris 9
France
Tel: +33 1 48 74 38 50

Musee Fragonard d'Alfort
Monstres, calculs et écorchés
Ecole Nationale Vétérinaire
d'Alfort
7, Avenue du Général de Gaulle
94704 Maisons-Alfort
Paris
France
Tel: +33 1 43 96 71 72

Venice
Ca Rezzonico
Museum of eighteenth-
century Venice
San Barnaba
Venice
Italy

Index

Acknowledgments

The photographer would like to thank all the people who so kindly allowed her into their homes
to take photographs for this book, in particular:

Austria:

Ernst Fuchs, Eva Fuchs, Stephan Riedl.

Belgium:

Thierry Bosquet, Christophe Decarpentrie, Agnes Emery, Christophe Vachére.

England:

Virginia Bates, Carolyn Corben, Duggie Fields, Nathalie Hambro,
Sera Hersham-Loftus, Peter Hone, Tim Knox and Tom Longstaff-Gowan,
Brian Lewis, Dennis Severs, Keith Skeel, Hassan Abdullah,
Stefan Karlson and Michel Lassere from Trois Garçons.

France:

Alexandre, Marie Beltrami, Brizio Bruschi, Vincent Darré, Amelie Dillmann,
Remy le Fur, Jacques Garcia, Michel Haillard, Philippe Model, Oddes, Pierre Peyrol,
Pierre et Gilles, David Rocheline, Ramuntcho de Saint Armand,
Hervé Thibault, Alexandre Vassiliev.

India:

Dimpel Kapadia.

Italy:

Antonio Presto, Franco Maria Ricci, Niki de Saint Phalle.

Morocco:

Comtesse Boul de Breteuil, Alessandra Lippini, Franca and Carla Sozzani, Bill Willis.

Portugal:

Francesco Capello.

Spain:

Ricardo Bofill.

USA:

Dianne Blell, Tony Duquette, Rick Ellis, Richard Gillettes, Ira Jaeger, Lisa Lou, Izhar Patkin, David
Roos, Ruth Shuman, Hunt Slonem, Michael Trapp, John Woodrow Kelley, Lillian Williams.

And also, of course, Stephen Calloway for a superb collaboration.

The authors and photographer would also like to thank the following people
for all their help, support, friendship, knowledge and hospitality:
Alexandra d'Arnoux, Emilio Bazone, Laurel Beizer, Michael Benevento, Linda Benglis,
Marie Claire Blanckaerdt, Mattia Bonetti, Mark Brazier Jones, Michèle Champenois,
Laurent de Commines, Eileen Coyne, Diane Dorrans Saeks, Fulvio Ferrari, Isabelle Forestier,
Renate Gallois Montbrun, Charles Gandee, Elisabeth Garouste, Christiane Germain, David Gill,
Chuck Hettinger, Min Hogg, Joseph Holtzmann, Eric d'Huart, Abu Jani and Sandeep Koshla,
Thomas Jayne, Jason Kantos, Larissa, Freddie Leita, Andrew Logan, Kiko Lopez, Marion McEvoy,
Susanne von Meiss, Tamar Oppenheimer, Ann Poirier, Jacques Pontasez, Andrée Putman,
Jonathan Reed, Sandra Rhodes, Mirella Ricciardi, Ingrid Ross, Anand Sarabai, Phillippe Seuillet
(with whom she shot several reportages), Holly Solomon, Pam Strayer, Sarah Stewart,
Rixa von Treuenfels, Suzanne Trocmé, Hutton Wilkinson.

Thanks also to the following people at Michell Beazley:
Lara Maiklem, Auberon Hedgecoe, Emily Wilkinson, Emma Clegg, Lynn Bryan,
Nancy Roberts, and Alex Wiltshire.